Copyright © 2014 by Robert Lawton

All Rights Reserved.

Cover design by Erika Deoudes

First Edition.

This book is dedicated to anyone who chases a dream,
in spite of everything.

"I never learned as much from my successes as I have from my failures and rejections.
REJECTED! affirms what William Goldman and I have suspected for years:
Nobody knows anything.
Most 'experts' certainly know precious little about the creative fires
that burn in all our souls.
The most encouraging book I've read in memory."
- Ed Begley, Jr.

Table of Contents

INTRODUCTION	4
ART	**5**
PRO TIPS	26
BUSINESS	**29**
PRO TIPS	33
BAD CALLS	34
FILM	**37**
A FEW WORDS ABOUT THE FILM SECTION:	38
IN PRAISE OF GARBAGE	**69**
PRO TIPS	72
BAD CALLS	73
MAVERICKS	**75**
PRO TIPS	81
BAD CALLS	82
MUSIC	**85**
PRO TIPS	101
PERFORMERS	**103**
PRO TIPS	107
SPORTS	**109**
PRO TIPS	112
TELEVISION	**113**
PRO TIPS	118
BAD CALLS	119
WRITERS	**121**
PRO TIPS	157
THE TAKEAWAY	158
ACKNOWLEDGEMENTS	160
NOTES	**161**

Introduction

"Can't act. Slightly bald. Also dances."

- RKO note, written after Fred Astaire's 1933 screen test.

That's the one, which started this whole thing for me.

I recall hearing about that misguided assessment of Astaire years ago and taking encouragement from it.

Supposedly, he later kept a framed copy in his Beverly Hills mansion to remind himself how far he'd come.

After receiving a rejection recently I thought about this note, written by some long forgotten "expert" who trivialized & misjudged the future legend.

I began thinking; there must be other successful people who encountered rejection before their work was eventually appreciated.

Turns out there were quite a few.

My hope is that at least *one* person out there will read these true stories of perseverance despite adversity and become inspired.

Or, at least a bit less discouraged.

If nothing else, know this:

If you have a burning passion to create something?

Anything.

And you encounter fierce resistance, rejection and ridicule?

You're not alone.

In fact, you're in very good company.

ART

"What would life be if we had no courage to attempt anything?"
- Vincent van Gogh

The Armory Show - (February 17, 1913 - March 15, 1913)

"That's not art!" - Theodore Roosevelt.

The first major exhibition of modern art in America was nothing short of revolutionary.

It introduced an astonished public and outraged critics to a radical new style of painting from the likes of Duchamp, Gauguin, Matisse, Picasso and Van Gogh.

The critics and much of the public, clearly weren't ready:

"The most hideous monstrosities ever perpetrated."

"Like visiting a lunatic asylum... filled with anarchistic monkeys."

"These men have seized upon the modern engine of publicity and are making insanity pay."
- The New York Times (March 16, 1913).

Henri Matisse – *Blue Nude* (1907)

Blue Nude was burned in effigy when The Armory Exhibit traveled to Chicago.

The Armory show is now seen as a major turning point in the history of art.

Many of the works displayed there have since become priceless masterpieces.

Francis Bacon (1909-1992)

"That man who paints those dreadful pictures"
– Margaret Thatcher

Bacon often doubted his own talent and destroyed much of his early work.

His *Crucifixion* (1933) was badly received, so he quit painting for 10 years.

While being rejected for a Surrealist Exhibition, he was told:
"Mr. Bacon, don't you realize a lot has happened in painting since the Impressionists?"

In a 1985 interview, he recalled his early poverty:

*"I had lost all my money and I had no canvases left, and so the few I had, I just turned them, and I found that the, that the, what is called the wrong side, the unprimed side of the canvas worked for me very much better. So I've always used them.
So it was just by chance that I had no money to buy canvases with."*

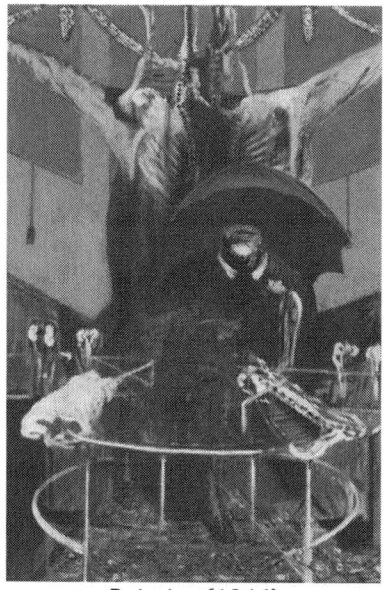

Painting (1946)

"Painting" sold for £200 in 1946.

In 2013, *Three Studies of Lucian Freud* sold for $142,405,000.

Paul Cézanne (1839-1906)

"Mr. Cézanne merely gives the impression of being a sort of madman, painting in a state of delirium tremens."
–Marc de Montifaud, L'Artiste (1874)

The enormously influential Paris Salon rejected Cézanne's submissions every year from 1864 to 1869.

He continued to submit works until 1882 when finally, through the intervention of a fellow artist, he exhibited his first and last successful submission there.

Cézanne - The Card Players (1894/95)

In 2012, *The Card Players* set a world record for the highest price ever paid for a single work of art - US $250 million.

"Cézanne was the father of us all."
- Pablo Picasso

Marcel Duchamp (1887-1968)

"A nude never descends the stairs, a nude reclines."
- Reason given for *Nude descending a staircase, No. 2*'s rejection by The Paris Salon.
Duchamp later said:
*"I took my painting home in a taxi.
It was really a turning point in my life, I can assure you.
I saw that I would not be very much interested in groups after that."*

When displayed at The Armory Show, *Nude No. 2* sparked a storm of controversy:

"It looks like an explosion in a shingle mill."
– The New York Times (February, 1913).

*"It looks like a pack of brown cards in a nightmare
or a dynamited suit of Japanese armor."*
- Chicago Daily Tribune (February, 1913).

"He is nuts and his imagination has gone wild!"
– Theodore Roosevelt (February, 1913).

Nude descending a staircase, No. 2 (1912)

The painting sold at The Armory Show for $324.
It is now regarded as one of the most significant pieces of modern art ever created.

Paul Gauguin (1848-1903)

In 1871, at the age of 23, Gauguin began painting in his free time.
In 1884, he moved with his wife and five children to Denmark,
where he pursued a career as a salesman.
He failed.
His family fell apart when he decided to become a full-time artist.

In 1888, van Gogh invited Gauguin to paint with him in Arles.
When Gauguin later chose to leave, a despondent van Gogh cut off his own ear.
They never saw each other again.

His last physical contact with his family was in 1891,
just before he sailed alone to French Polynesia:
"To escape everything that is artificial and conventional."

He battled depression and at least once attempted suicide.
In 1903, he was sentenced to prison for libeling the Governor.
Penniless, suffering from syphilis and alcoholism, Gauguin died at age 54.

Only later was Gauguin appreciated for his innovative style and bold use of colors.
His work proved to be enormously influential to artists like Picasso and Matisse.

His paintings are now rarely offered for sale.
Most are currently valued at around US $30 million each.

2 Tahitian Women (1899)

The Impressionists (c. 1870's-1880's)

The "Impressionists" were outcasts. Radicals.

In the late 19th century, people were accustomed to realistic art.
Typically portraits, historic or religious scenes where
"the painter's hand was hidden."

In Europe at this time, the only game in town was the juried "Salon de Paris"
if an artist wanted recognition for their work.

In the 1860's, a small group including Monet, Renoir and other Salon de Paris "rejects"
began working in a radical new style:
Using natural light, painting landscapes and contemporary life.

In 1863 Édouard Manet's *"The Luncheon on the Grass"* was one of 4,000 paintings rejected
by The Salon de Paris in that year alone.

In response, Salon des Refusés ("The Exhibition of Rejects") was organized.
It attracted more visitors than the regular Salon.

The artists petitioned for another Exhibition of Rejects in 1867 and again in 1872, but
were denied.

In 1874, artists including Cézanne, Pisarro, Renoir, Degas, Monet and Manet
held their own, independent exhibition.

The critical response was hostile.

One used the term *"Impressionist"* in his review.

It was intended as an insult.

*"Five or six lunatics, one of them a woman — a collection of unfortunates
tainted by the folly of ambition — have met here to exhibit their works.
What a terrifying spectacle is this of human vanity stretched to the verge of dementia."*
- Le Figaro

*"I confess humbly I do not see nature as they do, never having seen these skies fluffy with
pink cotton, these opaque and moiré waters, this multi-colored foliage.
Maybe they do exist. I do not know them."*
- Le Siècle

Claude Monet – *Impression, Sunrise* (1872)

"Wallpaper in its embryonic state is more finished than that seascape."
- Le Charivari (April 25, 1874)

Impression, Sunrise failed to sell at the Exhibition.

It is now considered priceless.

Camille Pissarro - *Landscape through trees* (1875)

"Someone should tell Monsieur Pissarro forcibly that trees are never violet, that the sky is never the color of fresh butter, that no sensible human being could countenance such aberrations and that nowhere on earth are things to be seen as he paints them."
- Le Figaro (1876)

Pierre-Auguste Renoir - *Nude in the Sun* (1875)

*"Try to explain to Monsieur Renoir that a woman's torso is not a mass of decomposing flesh
with those purplish green stains
which denote a state of complete putrefaction in a corpse."*
- Le Figaro (1876)

Gustav Klimt (1862-1918)

"If you cannot please everyone with your deeds and your art, please only a few. To please many is bad."
- Quote from Schiller used in Klimt's *Nuda Veritas (1899)*.

Klimt lived in poverty while attending art school.

In 1894, he was commissioned to create three paintings to decorate The Great Hall at the University of Vienna.

When completed, the paintings *Philosophy*, *Medicine*, and *Jurisprudence* were called "*pornographic*" and not displayed.

Adele Bloch-Bauer I (1907)

In 2006, his portrait, *Adele Bloch-Bauer I* was purchased for US $135 million.

This surpassed Picasso's *Boy With a Pipe* (sold in 2004, for $104 million) as the highest reported price ever paid for a single painting at the time.

Édouard Manet (1832-1883)

"The insults rain down on me like hail."

Manet enjoyed little acceptance or acclaim in his lifetime.

Yet, his revolutionary art contributed enormously to the rise of impressionism.

The Luncheon on the Grass (Le déjeuner sur l'herbe), (1863)

The Paris Salon's rejection of *The Luncheon in the Grass (1863)* and *Olympia (1863)* led directly to the first exhibition of impressionist art
- *The Salon de Refusés (Exhibition of Rejects).*

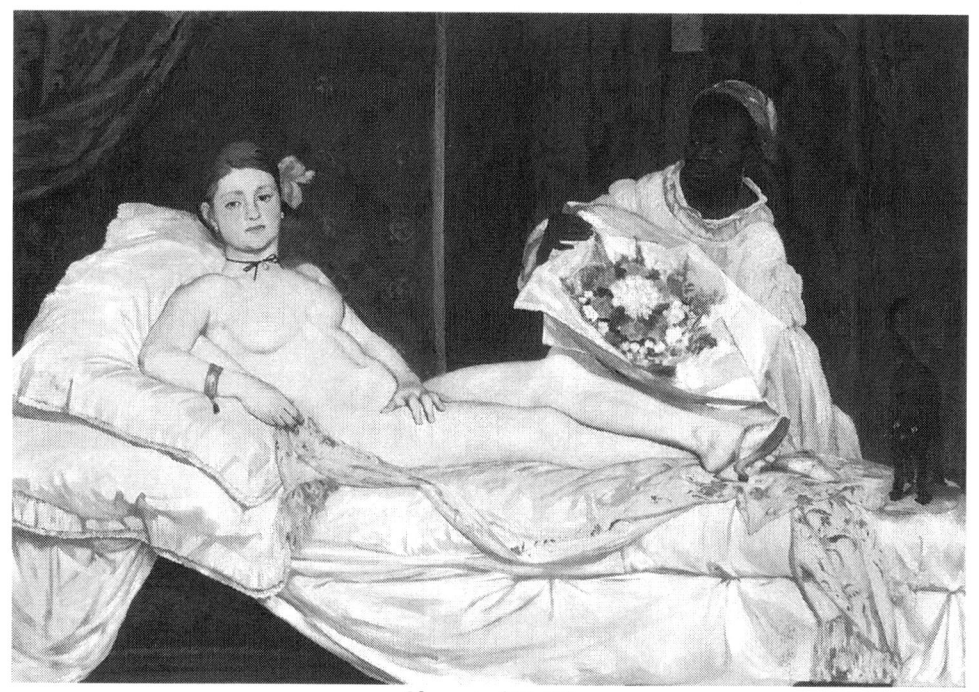

Olympia (1863)

Olympia caused a scandal when displayed in 1865.

Critics called it *"vulgar, immoral and obscene."*

"Art sunk so low doesn't even deserve reproach."
-La Presse

"What is this Odalisque with a yellow stomach, a base model picked up I know not where, who represents Olympia?"
–L'Artiste

"If the canvas of the Olympia was not destroyed, it is only the precautions taken by the administration prevented the painting being punctured and torn."
– Manet's friend, Antonin Proust

In 1881 (pressured by Antonin Proust) the French government awarded Manet the Legion of Honour, France's highest honor.

Olympia now hangs in the Louvre.

Henri Matisse (1869-1954)

"A pot of paint has been flung in the face of the public."
- Critic's review of his 1905 exhibition.

The Green Line (1905)

Much of Matisse's early work encountered vehement criticism and it was often difficult for him to provide for his family.

In response to his work at the 1913 Armory Show, one critic wrote:
*"We may as well say in the first place that his pictures are ugly,
that they are coarse, that they are narrow,
that to us they are revolting in their inhumanity."*
– The New York Times (February 23, 1913)

When The 1913 Armory Exhibition travelled to Chicago, students at the Chicago Art Institute burned his painting *Blue Nude (1907)* in effigy.

In 2005, New York's MoMA purchased *The Plum Blossoms* (1948) for $25 million.

Claude Monet (1840-1926)

"Age and chagrin have worn me out. My life has been nothing but a failure, and all that's left for me to do is to destroy my paintings before I disappear."
- From a letter to a friend.

Monet struggled with poverty, self-doubt and illness throughout his life.

His father wanted him to pursue a career in business,
but his mother supported his artistic efforts.
She died when he was 16.

When Monet visited the Louvre, he witnessed artists copying the displayed artwork. He chose to sit by a window instead, painting what he saw rather than copy others.

In 1867, he and his wife experienced great hardship around the birth of their son. His father, who disapproved of Monet being an artist, was unwilling to help.
He became so despondent that he attempted suicide,
trying to drown himself in The Seine River.

Monet often became frustrated with his work and is believed to have destroyed as many as 500 of his own paintings.

He died in 1926, never realizing how important he was.

Le Bassin Aux Nymphéas (1919)

In 2008, *Le Bassin Aux Nymphéas* sold for US $80 Million.

Pablo Picasso (1881-1973)

"One day we shall find Pablo has hanged himself behind his great canvas."
– André Derain after seeing Les Demoiselles.

In 1907, Picasso showed his latest painting *Les Demoiselles d'Avignon*
to a small group of friends at his studio.
Everyone hated it.

Matisse was angered by it, believing it to be a hoax.
Braque said: *"It's as if you are making us eat rope and drink turpentine."*
Dealer Ambroise Vollard lost interest in Picasso after seeing it.
One said: *"It was the ugliness of the faces that froze with horror the half-converted."*

Picasso rolled it up and it wasn't exhibited again until 1916.
It didn't sell until 1924, when it was bought sight-unseen.
In 1937, New York's MoMA bought it for their permanent collection.

Les Demoiselles d'Avignon (1907)

*"Les Demoiselles d'Avignon was a principal detonator of the modern movement.
The cornerstone of twentieth-century art."*
- Picasso biographer John Richardson (1991).

Pierre-Auguste Renoir (1841-1919)

"Had he learned to draw, Renoir would have made a very pleasing canvas out of his Luncheon of the Boating Party."
– Le Figaro (1882)

Luncheon of the Boating Party (1881)

As a leading figure in the Impressionist movement, Renoir was not spared derision from the prevailing opinion of his era.

Thankfully, he continued painting.

Renoir created several thousand paintings in his lifetime.

He painted Composer Richard Wagner's portrait in 35 minutes.
In 1883, he created fifteen paintings in one month.

When he first started as a painter, Renoir often couldn't afford to buy art supplies.

In 2009, one of his paintings sold for US $78 million.

Auguste Rodin (1840-1917)

"I have an idiot for a son!"
– His father, Jean-Baptiste Rodin

In 1857, Rodin attempted 3 times to gain admittance into Paris' Grand École.
He was rejected each time.

Rodin lived in poverty until his late 30's.

When he traveled to Italy in 1875, he discovered the work of Michelangelo,
whose work had a profound effect on him:
"It is Michelangelo who has freed me from academic sculpture."

Departing from convention, Rodin became a naturalist sculptor,
in contrast to the idealism of the Greeks.

In 1879, he began his most famous work: *The Thinker* and he is known today as
one of the most important sculptors in history.

Auguste Rodin – The Thinker (1879-1889)

Henri de Toulouse-Lautrec (1864-1901)

"I knew, papa, that you wouldn't miss the death."
- His last words, spoken to his father.

A close friend to Vincent van Gogh and Cézanne,
Toulouse-Lautrec had a very tough go of it while he lived.

In addition to struggling as an artist, he suffered from major physical disabilities and chronic health problems.

Often ridiculed for his appearance, Toulouse-Lautrec became an alcoholic.

He died from complications due to alcoholism and syphilis at the age of 36.

In 2005, his painting *La blanchisseuse* sold for US $22.4 million.

La blanchisseuse/The Laundress (1889)

Vincent van Gogh (1853-1890)

"Painting is a faith, and it imposes the duty to disregard public opinion."
- Vincent van Gogh

Van Gogh was a singularly talented genius whose brilliance went unrecognized while he lived.
Although he produced more than 2,000 works in his lifetime, he sold just one.
To a friend.

In February, 1886 he wrote his brother Theo to say that he could only recall:
"Eating six hot meals since the previous May."

He fatally shot himself at the age of 37.
His last words were:
"The sadness will last forever."

Self-portrait without beard (1889)

He gave his final self-portrait to his mother as a birthday gift.

Vincent van Gogh is now recognized as one of the greatest artists to have ever lived.

Johannes Vermeer (1632-1675)

On December 29, 1653 Vermeer became a member of a painter's trade association. He couldn't afford to pay the admission fee.

In 1675 he borrowed money, using his mother-in-law as a guarantor.

He died suddenly in December 1675, leaving his family in debt.

In a letter to creditors, his wife described how financial stress had killed him:

"He was unable to sell any of his art. As a result and owing to the great burden of his children, he lapsed into such decay that in a day and a half he went from being healthy to being dead."

For centuries after Vermeer's death, his work was ignored.

The Concert (1664), which was stolen in 1990, is now valued at more than $200,000,000.

Vermeer - The Milkmaid, (1657/58)

PRO TIPS

"A work of art which did not begin in emotion is not art."
- Paul Cézanne

"If I create from the heart, nearly everything works; if from the head, almost nothing."
- Marc Chagall

"Creativity takes courage."
- Henri Matisse

"I saw the angel in the marble and carved until I set him free"
- Michelangelo

"Art is the supreme task and the truly metaphysical activity in this life."
- Friedrich Nietzsche

"I found I could say things with color and shapes that I couldn't say any other way - things I had no words for."
- Georgia O'Keeffe

"The artist is a receptacle for emotions that come from all over the place: from the sky, from the earth, from a scrap of paper, from a passing shape, from a spider's web."
- Pablo Picasso

"Painting is the grandchild of nature. It is related to God."
- Rembrandt

"You come to nature with all her theories, and she knocks them all flat."
- Pierre Auguste Renoir

"The world of reality has its limits; the world of imagination is boundless."
- Jean-Jacques Rousseau

"Art is never finished, only abandoned."
- Paul Valéry

"If you hear a voice within you say 'you cannot paint,' then by all means paint and that voice will be silenced."
- Vincent van Gogh

"Don't think about making art, just get it done. Let everyone else decide if it's good or bad, whether they love it or hate it. While they are deciding, make even more art."
- Andy Warhol

THE MUSEUM OF MODERN ART
NEW YORK 19

11 WEST 53rd STREET
TELEPHONE: CIRCLE 5-8900
CABLES: MODERNART, NEW-YORK

THE MUSEUM COLLECTIONS

October 18, 1956

Dear Mr. Warhol:

Last week our Committee on the Museum Collections held its first meeting of the fall season and had a chance to study your drawing entitled <u>Shoe</u> which you so generously offered as a gift to the Museum.

I regret that I must report to you that the Committee decided, after careful consideration, that they ought not to accept it for our Collection.

Let me explain that because of our severely limited gallery and storage space we must turn down many gifts offered, since we feel it is not fair to accept as a gift a work which may be shown only infrequently.

Nevertheless, the Committee has asked me to pass on to you their thanks for your generous expression of interest in our Collection.

Sincerely,

Alfred H. Barr, Jr.
Director of the Museum Collections

Mr. Andy Warhol
242 Lexington Avenue
New York, New York

AHB:bj

P.S. The drawing may be picked up from the Museum at your convenience.

Andy Warhol's MoMA rejection

BUSINESS

"Fall down seven times, stand up eight."
- Japanese proverb

Chester Carlson (1906-1968)
He grew up poor, joining the workforce at age 8 and later worked his way through CalTech, but schoolwork prevented him from earning the full $260 annual tuition. By the time he graduated at the start of the Great Depression, he was $1,500 in debt. Carlson sought employment from 82 companies, but received no job offers.
By 1938, while working full time and attending law school, he worked on an invention for making copies. He hired an assistant, Otto Kornei and on October 22, 1938, they created the first xerographic copy.
Later, Kornei parted with Carlson and was so discouraged, he dissolved their agreement, which would have given him 10% of all future proceeds.
Over the next 5 years, Carlson was turned down for funding by 20 companies and tried to sell it outright to IBM, Kodak, Harris-Seybold and the Navy. They all passed.
After eight years of rejection, a tiny company called Haloid agreed to invest. They later changed their name to Xerox.
Fortune magazine later ranked Carlson as one of America's wealthiest citizens. He donated more than $150 million to charities in his lifetime.

Mark Cuban
He tried carpentry, was a short order cook, waited tables, tried to sell powdered milk and was fired as a software salesman.
He's now a billionaire and owns The Dallas Mavericks.
"I've learned that it doesn't matter how many times you failed, you only have to be right once. I was an idiot lots of times and I learned from them all."

Walt Disney (1901-1966)
"You lack imagination and have no good ideas."
- The reason given for Walt's being fired as a newspaper cartoonist.
His first animation company went bankrupt and Walt survived by eating dog food.
He later created a character named "Oswald the Rabbit" but his distributor Universal, assumed ownership and hired his artists away from under him.
When the film industry learned of Walt's plans to produce a full-length animated feature *"Snow White"*, he was lambasted and the project known as: *"Disney's folly."*
Snow White became the most successful film of 1938 and changed the industry.
Last year, The Walt Disney company revenues were $45 billion.

Henry Ford (1863-1947)
"Failure is simply an opportunity to begin again, this time more intelligently."
Ford neither invented the automobile nor the assembly line, but he perfected them. His early businesses failed, he went broke several times before becoming successful and he died as one of the wealthiest men in the world.

Chris Gardner
"You can only depend on yourself. The cavalry 'ain't coming." - Gardner's mother.
He grew up in foster care and was a homeless single parent before becoming a stockbroker. He later founded his own brokerage firm and became a philanthropist.

Bill Gates
"Success is a lousy teacher. It seduces smart people into thinking they can't lose."
Gates dropped out of Harvard to start a business called "Traf-O-Data".
It failed. He started over and is now one of the wealthiest people in the world.

Soichiro Honda (1906-1991)
At 15, with no formal education, Honda left home to look for work.
He obtained an apprenticeship at a garage and worked for six years as a mechanic.
Honda became unemployed and was rejected by Toyota for an engineer's job.
So he started making his own scooters at home.
Eventually, this became the multibillion-dollar Honda Motors.

Steve Jobs, (1955-2011)
*"The only way to do great work is to love what you do.
If you haven't found it yet, keep looking. Don't settle.
As with all matters of the heart, you'll know when you find it.
And, like any great relationship, it just gets better and better as the years roll on.
So keep looking until you find it. Don't settle."* - Stanford Commencement speech.
In 1985 Apple, the company he co-created, fired him.
He started another company, NeXT and then another, Pixar.
By 1996, Jobs returned as CEO to a struggling Apple.
He transformed it into one of the most valuable companies in the world.

Jack Ma
Born poor in China, Ma learned English by trading tours to tourists for lessons.
He failed a college entrance exam twice and was rejected 10 to 15 times for jobs.
In 1995, he started an internet company. It failed. He started another. It also failed. In 1999, he started AliBaba with $50k in loans. Ma is now the richest man in China.

R. H. Macy (1822-1877)
Macy started 7 businesses which all failed before his NYC store became successful. On the first day of operating (October 28, 1858) sales totaled $11.08.
In 2013, company revenues were nearly $30 billion.

Akio Morita (1921-1999)
Morita started Sony with a partner and $500.
Bulova ordered 100,000 of their radios, if they could be sold under the Bulova name.
Despite his partner instructing him to accept the order, Morita turned them down. He later said this was the best business decision of his career.

Sumner Redstone
"Great success is built on failure, frustration, even catastrophe."
In 1979, he survived a hotel fire by hanging outside of his third-story window.
He suffered third degree burns and was told he would never have a normal life.
He soon resumed playing tennis almost daily and has become a multi-billionaire.

Harland David Sanders/Colonel Sanders (1890-1980)

At an age when most people retire, Sanders was just starting over.
He had been a 6th-grade dropout, a farmhand, a mule-tender, a locomotive fireman, railroad worker, aspiring lawyer, insurance salesman, ferryboat entrepreneur, tire salesman, amateur obstetrician, political candidate and gas station/motel operator.
At the age of 65, a new interstate diverted traffic away from his business.
Sanders had only a $105 Social Security check and a "secret recipe" for fried chicken.
KFC was rejected 1,009 times before being accepted.
By 1980, there were 6,000 KFC's in 48 countries, with annual sales of $2 billion.

Steven Spielberg

Spielberg was twice rejected for admission by the USC Film School.
In 1994, USC offered him an honorary degree. Spielberg agreed to accept only if the admissions officer who had twice rejected him, signed it.

Ted Turner

Ted Turner lost a sister to illness and a father to suicide.
He received dual rejections as a teenager from Princeton and Harvard.
He attended Brown University before being expelled.
Turner took over the family business at age 24, after his father's suicide.
He built it into a multibillion-dollar media empire.
"I want to be sure to make this point: I did everything I did without a college degree."

Oprah Winfrey

Winfrey was born into poverty to a teenage single mother in rural Mississippi.
She often had to wear potato sacks as a child.
At 22, she was fired from her job as a television reporter after being told she was: *"Unfit for television news."*
Oprah is currently the only female African-American billionaire in North America.

F. W. Woolworth (1852-1919)

As a young man, Woolworth worked at a dry goods store but was forbidden from waiting on customers because his boss felt: *"He lacked the sense needed to do so."*
He borrowed $300 and opened a 5-cent store in 1878. It failed within weeks.
Woolworth opened a second store in 1879. By 1911, the Woolworth Company was incorporated with 586 stores.
When he died, he was worth the equivalent of 1/1214th of the entire U.S. GNP.

Nick Woodman

Woodman's first company ended in failure, resulting in a total loss to investors, so he chose to finance his next business by selling bracelets with his wife from a car.
GoPro, created from his desire to document his own surfing adventures has gone from a tiny company, to a multi-billion dollar public corporation in ten years.
Woodman currently has a personal net worth of more than a billion dollars.

PRO TIPS

"Don't worry about people stealing your ideas.
If your ideas are any good, you'll have to ram them down people's throats."
– Howard Aiken

"I knew that if I failed I wouldn't regret that,
but I knew the one thing I might regret is not trying."
- Jeff Bezos, Amazon founder and CEO

"There are no rules. You don't learn to walk by following rules. You learn by doing."
- Richard Branson

"Setbacks teach lessons that carry you along.
You learn that a temporary defeat is not a permanent one.
In the end, it can be an opportunity."
- Warren Buffett

"If you want to be happy, set a goal that commands your thoughts,
liberates your energy, and inspires your hopes."
- Andrew Carnegie

"You may not realize it when it happens,
but a kick in the teeth may be the best thing in the world for you."
- Walt Disney.

"Failure is success if we learn from it."
- Malcolm Forbes

"Whether you think that you can or you can't, you're usually right."
- Henry Ford

"Sometimes life will hit you in the head with a brick, don't lose faith."
– Steve Jobs

"The essential part of creativity is not being afraid to fail."
- Edwin Land

"If you want to succeed you should strike out on new paths,
rather than travel the worn paths of accepted success."
- John D. Rockefeller

"If I had thought about it, I wouldn't have done the experiment.
The literature was full of examples that said 'you can't do this.'"
- Spencer Silver, inventor of 3-M "Post-It" notes.

BAD CALLS

*"Rail travel at high speed is not possible,
because passengers, unable to breathe, would die of asphyxia."*
- Dr. Dionysys Lardner, London University College Professor (1823).

"Drill for oil? You mean drill into the ground to try and find oil? You're crazy."
- Workers response to Edwin L. Drake who later became the first oil driller in the United States (1859).

"Well-informed people know that it is impossible to transmit the human voice over wires as may be done with dots and dashes of Morse code, and that, were it possible to do so, the thing would be of no practical value."
- Boston newspaper (1865).

"This 'telephone' has too many shortcomings to be seriously considered as a means of communication. The device is inherently of no value to us."
- Western Union internal memo (1876).

"What use could this company make of an electrical toy?"
William Orton, Western Union Telegraph President after being offered the chance to buy the patent for the telephone (1876).

*"The Americans have need of the telephone, but we do not.
We have plenty of messenger boys."*
- Sir William Preece, British Post Office Chief (1876).

"The horse is here to stay but the automobile is only a novelty, a fad."
- Michigan Savings Bank president, when asked by Horace Rackham if he should invest in Henry Ford (1903).

"That the automobile has practically reached the limit of its development is suggested by the fact that during the past year no improvements of a radical nature have been introduced."
- Scientific American (1909).

*"The wireless music box has no imaginable commercial value.
Who would pay for a message sent to nobody in particular?"*
- Reply to radio pioneer David Sarnoff's urgings for investment in radio in the 1920s.

"Stocks have reached what looks like a permanently high plateau."
- Irving Fisher, Professor of Economics, Yale University (1929).

"There will never be a bigger plane built."
- Boeing engineer re; Boeing's 247, a plane which holds 10 passengers (1933).

"Computers in the future may weigh no more than 1.5 tons."
- Popular Mechanics (1949).

"It would appear we have reached the limits of what it is possible to achieve with computer technology."
- Computer Scientist John von Neumann (1949).

"Nuclear-powered vacuum cleaners will probably be a reality in 10 years."
- Alex Lewyt, president of Lewyt Vacuum Co. (1955).

"I have traveled the length and breadth of this country and talked with the best people, and I can assure you that data processing is a fad that won't last out the year."
- Prentice Hall business books editor (1957).

"There is practically no chance communications space satellites will be used to provide better telephone, telegraph, television, or radio service inside the United States."
–FCC Commissioner T. Craven (1961).

"The concept is interesting and well-formed, but in order to earn better than a 'C', the idea must be feasible."
- Yale professor re; Fred Smith's 1962 essay. Smith later founded FedEx.

"Remote shopping, while entirely feasible, will flop - because women like to get out of the house, like to handle merchandise, like to be able to change their minds."
- TIME Magazine (1966).

"With over 15 types of foreign cars already on sale here, the Japanese auto industry isn't likely to carve out a big share of the market."
- Businessweek Magazine (1968).

"There is no reason anyone would want a computer in their home."
- Ken Olsen, Digital Equipment Corp. founder (1977).

"A cookie store is a bad idea. Besides, the market research reports say America likes crispy cookies, not soft and chewy cookies like you make."
- Advice given to Debbi Fields re; starting Mrs. Fields' Cookies.

"You want to have consistent and uniform muscle development across all of your muscles? It can't be done. It's just a fact of life. You just have to accept inconsistent muscle development as an unalterable condition of weight training."
- Response to Arthur Jones, inventor of Nautilus.

"The Internet? Bah!"
- *"Why the Internet will Fail"* by Clifford Stoll, Newsweek (1995).

"I predict the Internet will soon go spectacularly supernova and in 1996 catastrophically collapse."
- Robert Metcalfe, 3Com founder (1995).

"Apple is already dead."
- Nathan Myhrvold, former Microsoft CTO (1997).

"Y2K is a crisis without precedent in human history."
- Edmund DeJesus (1998).

"Two years from now, spam will be solved."
- Bill Gates, Microsoft founder (2004).

"There's no chance that the iPhone is going to get any significant market share."
– Steve Ballmer, Microsoft CEO (2007).

"So we went to Atari and said, 'Hey, we've got this amazing thing, even built with some of your parts, what do you think about funding us?
Or we'll give it to you. We just want to do it. Pay our salary, we'll come work for you.' And they said, 'No.' So then we went to Hewlett-Packard, and they said,
'Hey, we don't need you. You haven't gotten through college yet.'"
- Apple founder Steve Jobs re; his and Woz's first personal computer.

FILM

"Nobody knows anything."
- **William Goldman**

A few words about the Film section:

Chances are, every movie that appears here had a tough time getting made at all.

There are countless stories of films being produced despite enormous obstacles and just as many books & blogs detailing each of them.

This section isn't about that.
It's about great movies, which received lousy reviews.

I confined the sources to mainstream critics or media outlets only.
(It's easy to find a bad review of a great film in some tiny newspaper or website).
Not here.

The reviews are mostly those which appeared when the film was initially released.
(It's too easy for critics to be influenced after history has weighed in).

I included a small section at the end called "In Praise of Garbage".
There, you'll see how the same "experts" who pilloried great films, loved crap films.

Two examples:

Armond White, 3-time chairman of The NY Film Critics Circle & Sundance/Tribeca juror:
HATED *There Will Be Blood.*
Yet, he apparently felt Adam Sandler's *Grown Ups* was *"A work of art."*

The N.Y. Times' Vincent Canby didn't like *The Godfather: Part II*
But he sure seemed to enjoy *Ghostbusters II.*

Shit like that.

Also, these reviews are typically sections taken from within a larger whole.
However, I didn't "cherry pick" nasty snippets from glowing reviews.
If it shows up here?
It's representative of the entire review it came from.

I occasionally removed ellipses for clarity, so long as it in no way interfered with or altered the substance of the review.

Finally:
I included Academy Awards®, where appropriate.

Alien (1979)
"Alien contains a couple of genuine jolts, a barrage of convincing special effects
and enough gore to gross out children of all ages.
What's missing is wit, imagination and the vaguest hint of human feeling."
– Frank Rich, Time Magazine

"An empty-headed horror movie, with nothing to recommend it beyond
the disco-inspired art direction and some handsome, if gimmicky, cinematography.
The science fiction trappings add little to the primitive conception,
which features a rubber monster running amok in a spaceship...
for the most part, things simply jump out and go 'boo!'
Instead of characters, the film has bodies."
- Dave Kehr, Chicago Reader

"Occasionally one sees a film that uses the emotional resources of movies with such utter
cynicism that one feels sickened by the medium itself.
Alien is so 'effective' it has practically turned me off movies altogether.
The movie is terrifying, but not in a way that is remotely enjoyable."
– David Denby, New York Magazine

Aliens (1986)
"To me Aliens is one extremely violent, protracted attack on the senses,
as surviving space explorer Sigourney Weaver again confronts the spiny, slithering
creatures who killed her buddies in the original film, Alien.
Toward the end, the film resorts to placing a young girl in jeopardy
in a pathetic attempt to pander to who knows what audience.
Some people have praised the technical excellence of Aliens.
Well, the Eiffel Tower is technically impressive,
but I wouldn't want to watch it fall apart on people for two hours."
– Gene Siskel, Chicago Tribune

All The President's Men (1976)
Four Academy Awards®, including Best Adapted Screenplay
"The film is a splendidly proficient production of a woefully deficient script.
For one thing, it is long on substantiating detail and short on real action.
A great deal of time is spent showing Bernstein (Hoffman) and Woodward (Redford)
hunting and pecking at high speed on late-model typewriters, cradling telephone receivers
between neck and shoulder. Bernstein and Woodward consume countless containers of
coffee, lose many hours of sleep, pore over extremely long lists of 'leads,' and ring
innumerable doorbells. But to the eye of the thriller addict, all this is mere atmosphere; it
doesn't make the blood leap. And the elements that might do that are not available. There
are no big scenes; no confrontations, no sudden illuminations. Indeed, there are no villains.
Every country must find its own way to cope with national shame, and our way is
characteristically American: we have packaged Watergate and are selling it at $4 a head.
I await the musical version."
- Robert Hatch, The Nation

Amadeus, (1984) Best Picture
"Amadeus plays like a monument to mediocrity."
- Michael Sragow, Baltimore Sun

American Beauty (1999) Best Picture
"Bland and nasty, American Beauty has the slightly stale feel of a family sitcom. There's too much dead air around the dialogue and the comic pacing is nonexistent. Mendes's harsh and hyperbolic, if not particularly funny, satire of suburban angst makes The Ice Storm seem a nuanced masterpiece.
Bleak as it is, American Beauty has a certain car-wreck fascination but, with all the rubbernecking, there's no narrative flow.
As studied as its title would suggest, this is one cold movie.
All elements do laboriously come together as the action finally congeals into drama and, amid moments of sexual truth, goes glacially over the top."
– J. Hoberman, Village Voice

Apocalypse Now (1979)
"Apocalypse Now wants to be something more than a kind of cinematic tone poem. Mr. Coppola himself describes it as 'operatic,' but this, I suspect, is a word the director hit upon after the fact.
Ultimately, Apocalypse Now is neither a tone poem nor an opera. It's an adventure yarn with delusions of grandeur, a movie that ends —in the all-too-familiar words of the poet Mr. Coppola drags in by the bootstraps—not with a bang, but a whimper."
– Vincent Canby, The New York Times

Arthur (1981)
"Overrated one-joke comedy which indulges Moore's perpetual drunk act. Some of the lines are funny, but how can one applaud a movie which relies so heavily on the novelty value of Gielgud as a bitter butler pronouncing profanities in a posh accent?"
- Time Out London

Back To The Future (1985)
"An Underpowered Trip:
If Back to the Future had been about the size of, say, Repo Man, it might have been one of those appealing films that begs to be adopted.
It's not. It's big, cartoonish and empty, with an interesting premise that is underdeveloped and overproduced."
– Sheila Benson, Los Angeles Times

Badlands (1974)
"Unfortunately, movies about banal people are often banal themselves."
– The San Francisco Examiner

"Badlands has no more depth than The Sugarland Express,
and I found its cold detachment offensive."
- Pauline Kael, The New Yorker

Bad Santa (2003)
"It rides a one-trick reindeer that tires well before the second reel,
and it mistakes crudity and cruelty for humour."
– Peter Howell, Toronto Star

"A frozen pile of reindeer droppings.
The cinematic equivalent to passing a kidney stone, Zwigoff's unholy foray into
'dark comedy' gives us a suicidal, sociopathic drunk slinging swear words
with a ferocity that would make Tony Montana wince."
- K.J. Doughton, Film Threat

"There simply aren't enough laughs in this Christmas comedy
- it's more like a stocking stuffed with lumps of coal."
- Steven Rea, Philadelphia Inquirer

Being There (1979)
"Ashby's direction is marred by the same softness that made
The Last Detail and Coming Home so morally bland.
What emerges in the end is a strange ambiguity of attitude to the American political system
and a hollow humour about cultural values. The cinema of cynicism, really."
-Time Out London

Best In Show (2000)
"The rather unoriginal satiric flaw becomes obvious, in most cases, within 30 seconds. The
film has little to do but repeat the same giant bull's eye gags
over and over again."
- Owen Gleiberman, Entertainment Weekly

Big (1985)
"Yet another comedy about a boy occupying a man's body.
The overall premise is milked for some mild titillation involving the hero's sexual innocence,
making one wonder if the genre's popularity might involve some deeply sublimated form of
kiddie porn—
arguably the distilled ideological essence of squeaky-clean Reaganism."
- Jonathan Rosenbaum, The Chicago Reader

The Big Lebowski (1998)
"The film doesn't seem to be about anything other than its own cleverness."
– Todd McCarthy, Variety

"This film feels completely haphazard,
thrown together without much concern for organizing intelligence.

That's because, despite concocting an incomprehensible plot that comes to include pornographers, anarchists and an avant-garde painter, the Coens don't seem to be very interested in it and haven't cared that the Dude is not only too laid-back to pay his rent, he's also too laid-back to function as a protagonist.
Without coherence, there is anarchy, and when the wealthy Lebowski barks to the Dude, 'What in God's holy name are you blathering about?' he's speaking for the audience as well as himself."
– Kenneth Turan, Los Angeles Times

Blade Runner (1982)

"They all plod along while sometimes dazzling, sometimes boring special effects whiz by and Ford's climactic confrontation with Hauer approaches.
Instead of tension building, though, things are grinding to a halt, including Hauer's gears. Better you should go down to your local foreign car garage and watch them repair a Porsche, if you want to see something really exotic."
– Ralph Novak, People Magazine

Blazing Saddles (1974)

"Blazing Saddles is every Western you've ever seen, turned upside down and inside out, braced with a lot of low burlesque, which is fine.
In retrospect, however, one remembers along with the good gags the film's desperate, bone-crushing efforts to be funny.
One remembers exhaustion, perhaps because you kept wanting it to be funnier than it was. Much of the laughter Mr. Brooks inspires is hopeful, before-the-gag laughter, which can be terribly tiring."
- Vincent Canby, The New York Times

Blood Simple (1985)

"Blood Simple has no sense of what we normally think of as reality, and it has no connections with experience.
It's not a great exercise in style, either."
–Pauline Kael, The New Yorker

Blue Velvet (1986)

"[Rossellini] is degraded, slapped around, humiliated and undressed in front of the camera. And when you ask an actress to endure those experiences, you should keep your side of the bargain by putting her in an important film."
- Roger Ebert, Chicago Sun-Times

"In Blue Velvet, everything is geared to create an impression—it gives the movie a juvenile, 'Wouldn't it be neat if...' quality.
Blue Velvet isn't about David Lynch's view of the world, it's about David Lynch; he isn't interested in communicating, he's interested in parading his personality. The movie doesn't progress or deepen, it just gets weirder, and to no good end."
-Paul Attanasio, The Washington Post

The Blues Brothers (1980)
"There isn't a moment of The Blues Brothers that wouldn't have been more enjoyable if it had been mounted on a simpler scale. Mr. Belushi and Mr. Aykroyd have only about three funny scenes during the course of a long bloated saga."
- Janet Maslin, The New York Times

Bonnie and Clyde (1967)
"Incongruously couples comedy with crime, in this biopic of Bonnie Parker and Clyde Barrow, a pair of Texas desperadoes who roamed and robbed the southwest and midwest during the bleak Depression days of the early 1930s. Conceptually, the film leaves much to be desired, because killings and the backdrop of the Depression are scarcely material for a bundle of laughs."
- Variety

"It is a cheap piece of bald-faced slapstick comedy that treats the hideous depredations of that sleazy, moronic pair as though they were as full of fun and frolic as the jazz-age cutups in Thoroughly Modern Millie. This blending of farce with brutal killings is as pointless as it is lacking in taste, since it makes no valid commentary upon the already travestied truth. And it leaves an astonished critic wondering just what purpose Mr. Penn and Mr. Beatty think they serve with this strangely antique, sentimental claptrap."
- Bosley Crowther, The New York Times

Bottle Rocket (1996)
"A grueling, numbing black hole."
- Mick LaSalle, The San Francisco Chronicle

Boogie Nights (1997)
"On top of some preposterous and near-fatal plotting errors, Anderson makes the mistake of creating too many characters (supporting stars Graham and Cheadle don't get enough to do, while William H. Macy is wasted for the sake of a punchline.)"
– Jeff Vice, Deseret News

Braveheart (1995) Best Picture
"Everybody knows that a non-blubbering clause is standard in all movie stars' contracts. Too bad there isn't one banning self-indulgence when they direct."
- TIME Magazine

"A stew of Hollywood clichés. Pure Hokum."
- Time Out London

"A rambling disappointment."
– The Washington Post

The Breakfast Club (1985)

"The offhand, knowing humor of Mr. Hughes' Sixteen Candles is supplanted here by a deadly self-importance, occasionally leavened with a well-timed gag or a memorable bit of teenage slang. There are some good young actors in The Breakfast Club, though a couple of them have been given unplayable roles. The five young stars would have mixed well even without the fraudulent encounter-group candor toward which The Breakfast Club forces them. Mr. Hughes, having thought up the characters and simply flung them together, should have left well enough alone."
- Janet Maslin, The New York Times

Bridesmaids (2011)

"This supposed great experiment in femme-com bears the distinct scars of having been 'fixed' -- out of fear or financial imperative -- by and for dudes."
- Karina Longworth, The Village Voice

"By the time two hours had dragged by, I felt a lot like I had sat through a five-hour wedding."
– Lou Lumenick, NY Post

"Bridesmaids sorely lacks the saving grace of being consistently funny."
– Joe Leydon, Variety

"It's an overly contrived jumble, trying out too many comic ideas that eventually swamp the central subject of what a modern young woman expects regarding friendship, courtship and marriage."
– Armond White, New York Press

Butch Cassidy & The Sundance Kid (1969)

"Butch Cassidy and the Sundance Kid must have looked like a natural on paper, but, alas, the completed film is slow and disappointing. William Goldman's script is constantly too cute and never gets up the nerve, by God, to admit it's a Western. Goldman has his heroes saying such quick, witty and contemporary things that we're distracted: it's as if, in 1910, they were consciously speaking for the benefit of us clever 1969 types. This dialog is especially inappropriate in the final shoot-out, when it gets so bad we can't believe a word anyone says. And then the violent, bloody ending is also a mistake; apparently it was a misguided attempt to copy Bonnie & Clyde but the ending doesn't belong on Butch Cassidy, and we don't believe it and we walk out of the theater wondering what happened to that great movie we were seeing until an hour ago."
– Roger Ebert, Chicago Sun-Times

"'I got vision' brags Butch Cassidy, 'and the rest of the world wears bifocals.' Unfortunately, the rest of the world includes the makers of Butch Cassidy and the Sundance Kid. Every character, every scene, is marred by the film's double view, which oscillates between sympathy and farce." – TIME Magazine

Caddyshack (1980)
"Caddyshack never finds a consistent comic note of its own, but it plays host to all sorts of approaches from its stars, who sometimes hardly seem to be occupying the same movie. Caddyshack feels more like a movie that was written rather loosely, so that when shooting began there was freedom, too much freedom, for it to wander off in all directions in search of comic inspiration."
– Roger Ebert, Chicago Sun-Times

Casablanca (1942) Best Picture/Director/Screenplay
"The love story that takes us from time to time into the past is horribly wooden, and clichés everywhere lower the tension."
- William Whitebait, The New Statesman

"Nothing short of an invasion could add much to Casablanca."
- TIME Magazine

The Casablanca Experiment (see also; The *Steps* Experiment):

As an experiment in 1982, writer Chuck Ross re-typed the Casablanca script, changed the title to "Everybody Comes to Rick's" and submitted it to literary agencies as an original script under a pseudonym.
Some agencies wouldn't read it unsolicited. Others recognized it.
Many rejected it. The rejections included:

"I just think you need to rework it... you have excessive dialogue at times."

"I think the dialogue could have been sharper and I think the plot had a tendency to ramble. It could've been tighter and there could have been a cleaner line to it."

"I gave you five pages to grab me -- didn't do it."

"Too much dialogue, not enough exposition, the story line was weak, and in general didn't hold my interest."

"Story line is thin. Too much dialogue for amount of action. Not enough highs and lows in the script."

"I strongly recommend that you leaf through a book called Screenplay by Syd Field, especially the section pertaining to dialogue. This book may be an aid to you in putting a professional polish on your script, which I feel is its strongest need."

Chinatown (1974) Best Original Screenplay
"As much as I admire the work of both Polanski and Nicholson, I found Chinatown tedious from beginning to just before the end."
- Gene Siskel, Chicago Tribune

"The most acclaimed private-eye saga since The Big Sleep has the torpor of a wake.
Evans and Polanski are masters of Hollywood 'dramatic organization.
They ram home what they see as major points.
Chinatown brings to question not only their lack of subtlety, but their hypocrisy.
Polanski never favors compassion over carnage.
He has none of Towne's emotional stakes in the film.
Polanski smothers Towne's script. He never lets in any air. Polanski revels in artifice."
- Michael Sragow, New York Magazine

A Clockwork Orange (1971)

"A Clockwork Orange manifests itself on the screen as a painless, bloodless,
and ultimately pointless futuristic fantasy.
The first third splashes out of a wide-angle lens like a madly mod picture-spread
for Look magazine where Kubrick toiled briefly long, long ago.
The middle third provides a moderately engrossing indictment of B. F. Skinnerism in action.
But the last third of the movie is such a complete bore that even audiences of confirmed
Kubrickians have drowned out smatterings of applause with prolonged hissing.
But don't take my word for it.
See for yourself and suffer the damnation of boredom."
- Andrew Sarris, Village Voice

"A Clockwork Orange is an ideological mess,
a paranoid right-wing fantasy masquerading as an Orwellian warning.
We'll probably be debating A Clockwork Orange for a long time -- a long, weary and
pointless time. And a lot of people will go, if only out of curiosity. Too bad.
In addition to the things I've mentioned above -- things I really got mad about –
A Clockwork Orange commits another, perhaps even more unforgivable, artistic sin.
It is just plain talky and boring."
– Roger Ebert, Chicago Sun-Times

Clueless (1995)

"Clueless has a meandering plot that has something to do with Cher doing nice things for
people — if they're wearing the right clothes, that is — and searching for the one,
perfect guy to whom she can give her virginity.
The mixture of Heathers and Sandra Dee doesn't quite wash;
it's like biting into a tamale and finding it filled with Marshmallow Fluff.
What's more, the characters are so scrubbed of individuality that it's never
remotely clear which guy Cher should end up with.
She finally falls for her stepbrother (Paul Rudd), a twist so bizarre it makes you wonder if
Heckerling is warming up for The Soon-Yi Previn Story.
Then again, this lover boy is such a bland mensch — to me, he looked like a real Barney —
that even the vague whiff of symbolic incest carries no weight.
There was more heat passing between Greg and Marcia Brady."
—Owen Gleiberman, Entertainment Weekly

Die Hard (1988)

"It's when we get to some of the unnecessary adornments of the script that the movie shoots itself in the foot. The filmmakers introduce a gratuitous and unnecessary additional character: the deputy police chief (Paul Gleason), who doubts that the guy on the other end of the radio is really a New York cop at all.
As nearly as I can tell, the deputy chief is in the movie for only one purpose: to be consistently wrong at every step of the way and to provide a phony counterpoint to Willis' progress. The character is so willfully useless, so dumb, so much a product of the Idiot Plot Syndrome, that all by himself he successfully undermines the last half of the movie. Thrillers like this need to be well-oiled machines, with not a single wasted moment. Inappropriate and wrongheaded interruptions reveal the fragile nature of the plot and prevent it from working. Without the deputy chief and all that he represents, Die Hard would have been a more than passable thriller. With him, it's a mess."
- Roger Ebert, Chicago Sun-Times

"Add a percussive, big-star performance to the state-of-the-art mechanics, turn up all the knobs, and you've got a sure-fire, big-bucks, major-studio-style summer attraction. All that's left is to light the fuse. So why am I not having fun?"
- Hal Hinson, Washington Post

"First there was Sylvester Stallone, then came Arnold Schwarzenegger, and now—Bruce Willis. Bruce Willis? Not exactly a name that springs immediately to mind when thinking of muscles 'n' mayhem movies.
But such distinctions mean little to the perpetrators of Die Hard, the noisiest, ugliest, and most relentlessly stupid movie of the year."
– David Ehrenstein, Los Angeles Herald Examiner

Dirty Dancing (1987)

"The movie plays like one long, sad, compromise; it places packaging ahead of ambition."
- Roger Ebert

"The dance finale between Gray and Swayze, although an obvious crowd-pleaser, is performed to a contemporary song clearly intended for the charts, which blows the period feel right off the dance floor."
– Desson Thomson, Washington Post

Dog Day Afternoon (1975) Best Original Screenplay

"Sidney Lumet's direction raises the old Antonioni question: does a film about boredom have to be boring?
Enjoyable and even exciting at the start, Dog Day Afternoon degenerates into frustration and tedium toward nightfall— an experience no less painful for the audience than for the actors."
– Dave Kehr, Chicago Reader

Double Indemnity (1944)
"The very toughness of the picture is also weakness of its core, and the academic nature of its plotting limits its general appeal. The principal characters--an insurance salesman and a wicked woman, which Mr. MacMurray and Miss Stanwyck play— lack the attractiveness to render their fate of emotional consequences. And the fact that the story is told in flashback disposes its uncertainty."
– Bosley Crowther, The New York Times

Duck Soup (1933)
"Those mad clowns, the Marx brothers, are now holding forth on the Rivoli screen in their latest concoction, Duck Soup, a production in which the bludgeon is employed more often than the gimlet. The result is that this production is, for the most part, extremely noisy without being nearly as mirthful as their other films."
- The New York Times

Easy Rider (1969)
"Hopper, Fonda and their friends went out into America looking for a movie and found instead a small, pious statement (upper case) about our society (upper case), which is sick (upper case). It's pretty but lower case cinema."
-Vincent Canby, The New York Times

The Elephant Man (1980)
"I kept asking myself what the film was really trying to say about the human condition as reflected by John Merrick, and I kept drawing blanks. The film's philosophy is this shallow: (1) Wow, the Elephant Man sure looked hideous, and (2) gosh, isn't it wonderful how he kept on in spite of everything?"
– Roger Ebert, Chicago Sun-Times

The Empire Strikes Back (1980)
"Confession: When I went to see The Empire Strikes Back I found myself glancing at my watch. The Force is with us, indeed, and a lot of it is hot air. It's a measure of my mixed feelings about The Empire Strikes Back that I'm not at all sure that I understand the plot. The Empire Strikes Back is about as personal as a Christmas card from a bank."
- Vincent Canby, The New York Times

"The Empire Strikes Back is malodorous offal. Stale, limp, desperately stretched out, and pretentious. Infantile is the operative word. This witless banality is made even less bearable by the nonacting of the principals. Harrison Ford (Han) offers loutishness for charm and becomes the epitome of the interstellar drugstore cowboy. Mark Hamill (Luke) is still the talentless Tom Sawyer of outer space – wide-eyed, narrow-minded, strait-laced. Worst of all is Carrie Fisher, whose Leia is a cosmic Shirley Temple but without the slightest acting ability or vestige of prettiness. Though still very young, she looks, without recourse to special effects, at least fifty – the film's only true, albeit depressing, miracle."
– John Simon, National Review

Erin Brockovich (2000) Best Actress
"There is obviously a story here, but Erin Brockovich doesn't make it compelling. The film lacks focus and energy, the character development is facile and thin and what about those necklines?"
- Roger Ebert, Chicago Sun-Times

Fargo (1996) Best Actress/Original Screenplay
"The filmmakers Joel and Ethan Coen have apparently never got over the giggle value of their regional dialect. Fargo, their derisive new true-crime comedy, could be subtitled How to Laugh at People Who Talk Minnesotan."
- Richard Corliss, TIME

"VIOLENT FARGO A BRUTALLY UNFUNNY SATIRE: From the camera angles to the set design, everything is calculated to make the viewer feel superior to the cloddish, geeky characters on display."
– Dave Kehr, NY Daily news

Fight Club (1999)
"'It's only after we've lost everything that we're free to do anything,' Tyler Durden says, sounding like a man who tripped over the Nietzsche display on his way to the coffee bar in Borders. Fight Club is a thrill ride masquerading as philosophy. The kind of ride where some people puke and others can't wait to get on again."
- Roger Ebert, Chicago Sun-Times

"David Fincher's brutal shock show floats the idiotic premise that a modern-day onslaught of girly pop-cultural destinations (including IKEA and support groups) has resulted in a generation of spongy young men unable to express themselves as fully erect males. If, as Fincher has said, this is supposed to be funny, then the joke's on us."
– Lisa Schwarzbaum, Entertainment Weekly

The French Connection (1971) Best Picture/Actor/Director/Editing
"An urban crime thriller which won undeserved acclaim for its efficient but unremarkable elevated-railway chase and its clumsy, showy emphasis on grainy, sordid realism. The performances are strong, although Hackman has done far better than this portrayal of a hard-nosed cop obsessively tracking down a narcotics ring in New York, using methods disapproved of by his superiors. The real problems, however, are that Friedkin's nervy, noisy, undisciplined pseudo-realism sits uneasily with his suspense-motivated shock editing; and that compared to (say) Siegel's Dirty Harry, the film maintains no critical distance from (indeed, rather relishes) its 'loveable' hero's brutal vigilante psychology."
-Time Out London

The Fugitive (1993)
"The film treats this profoundly preposterous plot as if it were a serious idea."
– People Magazine

"Although I wasn't actually counting, I doubt that Ford has more than a couple of dozen lines of dialogue in this entire continuous-motion picture - a production that depends much more on flash and dash than on repartee. The Fugitive is pretty much one breathless pursuit after another. And even when nobody's actually running, the film is edited with breathless music-video pacing: No shot is held longer than a few seconds - the attention span of the average hummingbird, or pre-teen."
– Orlando Sentinel

Full Metal Jacket (1987)
"Kubrick seems to want to tell us the story of individual characters, to show how the war affected them, but it has been so long since he allowed spontaneous human nature into his films that he no longer knows how. After the departure of his two most memorable characters, the sergeant and the tubby kid, he is left with no characters (or actors) that we really care much about. And in a key scene at the end, when a marine feels joy after finally killing someone, the payoff is diminished because we don't give a damn about the character."
- Roger Ebert, Chicago Sun-Times

Gandhi, (1982)
Best Picture/Actor/Director/Screenplay
"It is too bad Gandhi doesn't have much resonance or insight to match its dignity. As it stands, the film is more stuffy than stately, more prestigious than prodigious. It never quite captures the essence of Gandhi, or the influence he exerted on other leaders, including Martin Luther King. It's a broad but shallow river of information."
- David Sterritt, Christian Science Monitor

Ghostbusters (1984)
"This film hasn't gotten very far past the idea stage. Its jokes, characters and story line are as wispy as the ghosts themselves, and a good deal less substantial. There is more attention to special effects than to humor."
– Janet Maslin, The New York Times

"Only intermittently impressive."
- Variety

Ghost World (2001)
"I didn't expect Rebecca of Sunnybrook Farm, but there's a limit to the mean-spiritedness one can endure in a character one is supposed to find delightful."
– Andrew Sarris, New York Observer

Gladiator (2000) Best Picture/Actor
"Grandiose and silly, Gladiator suggests what would happen if someone made a movie of the imminent extreme-football league and shot it as if it were a Chanel commercial."
– Elvis Mitchell, The New York Times

"Gladiator is being hailed by those with short memories as the equal of Spartacus
and Ben-Hur. This is more like Spartacus Lite. Or dark.
Phoenix is passable as Commodus, but a quirkier actor could have had more fun in the role.
Gladiator lacks joy. It employs depression as a substitute for personality and believes that if
the characters are bitter and morose enough, we won't notice how dull they are."
- Roger Ebert, Chicago Sun-Times

The Godfather Part II (1974)
Best Picture/Director/Supporting Actor/Adapted Screenplay
"The Godfather Part II is not very far along before one realizes
that it hasn't anything more to say. Looking very expensive but spiritually desperate,
it has the air of a very long, very elaborate revue sketch. Nothing is sacred.
Mr. Pacino, so fine the first time out, goes through the film looking glum,
sighing wearily as he orders the execution of an old associate or a brother,
winding up very lonely and powerful, which is just about the way he wound up before.
Mr. De Niro, one of our best young actors, is interesting as the young Vito until,
toward the end of his section of the film,
he starts giving a nightclub imitation of Mr. Brando's elderly Vito.
The only remarkable thing about Francis Ford Coppola's The Godfather, Part II
is the insistent manner in which it recalls how much better his original film was.
Also written by Mr. Coppola and Mario Puzo, it's not a sequel in any engaging way.
It's not really much of anything that can be easily defined.
It talks. It moves in fits and starts but it has no mind of its own.
Occasionally it repeats a point made in The Godfather (organized crime is just another kind
of American business) but its insights are fairly lame at this point.
Everything of any interest was thoroughly covered in the original film,
but like many people who have nothing to say, Part II won't shut up.
Even if Part II were a lot more cohesive, revealing and exciting than it is, it probably would
have run the risk of appearing to be the self-parody it now seems."
- Vincent Canby, The New York Times

Gone With The Wind (1939)
8 Oscars®, including Best Screenplay
"And how badly written it is! There is hardly a sharp or even a credible line.
It is picture-postcard writing, as it is picture-postcard photography
(and, for that matter, picture-postcard music).
As Ms. Scarlett, Vivien Leigh gives a thin and shallow performance.
She does not enrich the part by the slightest idiosyncrasy or originality.
Only Clark Gable, though one wearies of the knowing smile with which he monitors
Scarlett's escapades, triumphs over the banal lines through a pleasantly cynical conception
of the role and a hard, florid masculinity.
Perhaps in another thirty years GWTW may acquire its patina.
For the moment, at least to this unregenerate viewer, it is a bore."
- Arthur Schlesinger, Jr., The Atlantic

The Good, The Bad and The Ugly (1966)

"The third in the Clint Eastwood series of Italo westerns, The Good, the Bad and the Ugly is exactly that – a curious amalgam of the visually striking, the dramatically feeble and the offensively sadistic. Ennio Morricone's insistent music and Carlo Simi's baroque art direction further contribute to the pic's too-muchness."
– Variety

"Director Leone doesn't seem to care very much, and after 161 minutes of mayhem, audiences aren't likely to either."
- TIME Magazine

Goodfellas (1990)

"You have this friend who invites you over to see his barrel of weasels. He picks up the lid, and there they are—weasels, all right, snarling, biting, devouring each other, squirming around in a muck of their own making. After a very short while you would confirm for yourself that weasels were wretched, pathetic, disgusting, trivial creatures and, in fact, not all that interesting. The chances of your wanting to watch them for two and a half hours are slim. But with this long film, director Martin Scorsese acts as if the vile lives of some New York City organized crime types are worth scrutinizing. While Scorsese generates vivid images, he covered this ground in the superb Mean Streets in 1973. Here there's nothing to learn, nobody to sympathize with. Seen one weasel, seen 'em all."
– Ralph Novak, People Magazine

"Goodfellas is Martin Scorsese's colorful but dramatically unsatisfying inside look at Mafia life in 1955–1980 New York City."
- Joseph McBride, Variety

The Goonies (1985)

"So overloaded with Freudian imagery that the good doctor himself might feel embarrassed. A bunch of 13-year-old boys penetrate a secret cave in search of hidden treasure, and when they aren't squeezing through tight places or being doused with water, they're castrating statues or kicking villains in the crotch. References to Mark Twain, Warner Brothers swashbucklers, and the Our Gang comedies hover in the background, but despite these honorable sources, it's a charmless exercise: director Richard Donner turns the kids into shrieking ferrets, and his jumpy cutting seems to lag behind the action deliberately in a curious attempt to make the film seem more chaotic and cluttered. The usual Spielberg rhetoric about the sanctity of childhood and the beauty of dreams seems wholly factitious in this crass context, which even includes a commercial in the form of a rock video for the tie-in merchandise."
- Dave Kehr, The Chicago Reader

The Graduate (1967)
"The screenplay, which begins as genuine comedy, soon degenerates into spurious melodrama."
- TIME Magazine

The Great Dictator (1940)
"Through no fault of Chaplin's, during the two years he was at work on the picture, dictators became too sinister for comedy."
– TIME Magazine

Groundhog Day (1993)
"The situation is ripe with comic potential but the script provides more chuckles than belly laughs. Some sequences are crisply paced and comically terse, some ramble and others just plain don't work."
- Variety

Guess Who's coming to Dinner (1967)
"A leaden and stilted affair. A wishy-washy, sanctimonious plea for tolerance, directed with Kramer's customary verbosity and stodginess."
- Time Out London

The Hangover (2009)
"Early in this unraveling adventure, a Vegas tourist quips, 'Some guys just can't handle Vegas.' Yeah, we know a couple: writers Jon Lucas and Scott Moore."
– Lisa Kennedy, Denver Post

"An intriguing, time-hopping set-up is wasted on obnoxious characters, celebrity cameos and crass attempts at humour. It doesn't help that the central cast is almost entirely forgettable, from the smug lounge lizardry of Bradley Cooper to the boisterous Jack Black-lite of Zach Galifianakis. A genuine star – Vaughn, Rudd, either Wilson brother – would have made these characters likeable, rather than simply pitiful and tiring."
- Time Out London

Harold and Maude (1972)
"Death can be as funny as most things in life, I suppose, but not the way Harold and Maude go about it. And so what we get, finally, is a movie of attitudes. Harold is death, Maude life, and they manage to make the two seem so similar that life's hardly worth the extra bother. The visual style makes everyone look fresh from the Wax Museum, and all the movie lacks is a lot of day-old gardenias and lilies and roses in the lobby, filling the place with a cloying sweet smell. Nothing more to report today."
- Roger Ebert, Chicago Sun-Times

Heathers (1989)
"This misanthropic black comedy about the cruelty of high school teenagers succeeds at least in being offbeat, but its inanities and glib pretensions are so thick that it mainly comes across as tacky and contrived. The dialogue is relentlessly fancy without being witty, and the specious moralizing of the plot looks like it was tacked on to appease square adults; the real narrative force behind this movie is nihilist camp, as in Roger Corman's 1966 The Wild Angels but without the same degree of filmmaking skill.
If you're in a low mood, you might find it funny in spots."
- Jonathan Rosenbaum, The Chicago Reader

Home Alone (1990)
"The movie is quite enjoyable as long as it explores the fantasy of a neglected little boy having an entire house of his own to explore and play in, but the physical cruelty that dominates the last act leaves a sour taste, and the multiple continuity errors strain one's suspension of disbelief to near the breaking point."
- Jonathan Rosenbaum, The Chicago Reader

The Incredibles (2004)
"The Incredibles announces the studio's arrival in the vast yet overcrowded Hollywood lot of eardrum-bashing, metal-crunching action sludge."
- Jessica Winter, Village Voice

"Bird and the Pixar whizzes do what they do excellently;
you just wish they were doing something else."
– Atlanta Journal Constitution

Inglorious Basterds (2009)
"Inglourious Basterds is not boring, but it's ridiculous and appallingly insensitive."
- David Denby, The New Yorker

"The only hope for Inglourious Basterds is that audiences will embrace it the way the Broadway crowd did Springtime for Hitler: because it's so bad they think it's good."
– Michael Sragow, The Baltimore Sun

"Rarely has one of his movies felt as interminable as this one."
– Manohla Dargis, The New York Times

In Bruges (2008)
" A gruesome, confused stumblebum of a movie."
- Rex Reed, New York Observer

Jaws (1975)
"The characters, for the most part, and the non-fish elements in the story, are comparatively weak and not believable. When the fear level drops off, for example, you'll begin questioning the realism of how this little town fights the fish that threatens to close its beaches and thereby destroy its summer tourist economy.

*You'll wonder why they don't ultimately call in the Coast Guard, and you'll wonder, when it comes to killing the fish, why three men have to risk their necks.
Why doesn't somebody just get a big mother of a gun and blow the shark out of the water?"*
- Gene Siskel, Chicago Tribune

"It is a coarse-grained and exploitive work which depends on excess for its impact. Ashore it is a bore, awkwardly staged and lumpily written."
- Charles Champlin, Los Angeles Times

"The ads show a gaping shark's mouth. If sharks can yawn, that's presumably what this one was doing. It's certainly what I was doing all through this picture.
The direction is by Steven Spielberg, who did the unbearable Sugarland Express.
At least here he has shucked most of his arty mannerisms and has progressed almost to the level of a stock director of the '30s — say, Roy del Ruth."
– Stanley Kauffman, The New Republic

Jurassic Park (1993)

"The carnivorous dinos are efficient, resourceful predators: good scream-generators, in movie terms, because they're both intelligent and relentless, like the best serial killers. But neither they nor the placid herbivores inspire anything close to awe, even with the aid of audience stimulants like surging symphonic music (by the shameless John Williams) and repeated close-ups of wide-eyed, openmouthed actors.
The screenplay, which is credited to Michael Crichton and David Koepp, reduces Crichton's intricately constructed novel to its bare bones: people running away from hungry animals.
Spielberg's monsters have a showroom shine, but the novelty wears off fast; for all the ingenuity of the movie's engineering, Jurassic Park doesn't have the imagination—or the courage—to take us any place we haven't been a thousand times before. It's just a creature feature on amphetamines."
- Terrence Rafferty, The New Yorker

The King Of Comedy (1983)

"The King of Comedy is a royal disappointment.
To be sure, Robert De Niro turns in another virtuoso performance for Martin Scorsese, just as in their four previous efforts. But once again – and even more so – they come up with a character that it's hard to spend time with.
Even worse, the characters – in fact, all the characters – stand for nothing."
– Variety

"De Niro in disguise denies his characters a soul. [His] 'bravura' acting in Mean Streets, Taxi Driver and New York, New York collapsed into 'anti-acting' after he started turning himself into repugnant flesh eggies of soulless characters.
Pupkin is a nothing."
– Pauline Kael

Lawrence Of Arabia (1962) Best Picture/Director

"It is such a laboriously large conveyance of eye-filling outdoor spectacle—
such as brilliant display of endless desert and camels and Arabs and sheiks and skirmishes
with Turks and explosions and arguments with British military men—
that the possibly human, moving T. E. Lawrence is lost in it.
We know little more about this strange man when it is over than we did when it begins.
The fault seems to lie, first in the concept of telling the story of this self-tortured man
against a background of action that has the characteristic of a mammoth Western film.
The nature of Lawrence cannot be captured in grand Super-Panavision shots of sunrise on
the desert or in scenes of him arguing with a shrewd old British general in a massive
Moorish hall. The fault is also in the lengthy but surprisingly lusterless dialogue of Robert
Bolt's over-written screenplay. Seldom has so little been said in so many words...
sadly, this bold Sam Spiegel picture lacks the personal magnetism, the haunting strain of
mysticism and poetry that we've been thinking all these years would be dominant when a
film about Lawrence the mystic and the poet was made.
It reduces a legendary figure to conventional movie-hero size amidst magnificent and exotic
scenery but a conventional lot of action-film clichés."
- Bosley Crowther, The New York Times

The Life Aquatic, With Steve Zissou (2004)

"This is one of the most irritating, self-conscious and smug films of the year,
working neither as a dark comedy nor a character study."
– Richard Roeper

Little Miss Sunshine (2006) Best Original Screenplay

"Aint no Sunshine; Little Miss Sunshine is a rickety vehicle that travels mostly downhill. The
latest in a long line of Sundance clunkers."
– Jim Ridley, The Village Voice

"The most concentrated hit of Sundance pain since Pieces of April, Little Miss Sunshine was a
curdled apotheosis of the festival's favorite genre: the dysfunctional family road trip.
This particular clan consists of a motivational-speaker dad, a harried mom,
a tubby seven-year-old would-be beauty queen, a Nietzsche-reading teenage son,
a heroin-snorting, foul-mouthed granddad and a suicidal Proust-scholar uncle.
The destination is a pageant that will demonstrate, in grotesque, stomach-churning detail,
that beauty is skin-deep and that you don't have to win to be a winner."
- Dennis Lim, Village Voice

Mad Max (1979)

"Viciously violent and awfully shallow."
- The Christian Science Monitor

"Mad Max is ugly and incoherent, and aimed, probably accurately,
at the most uncritical of moviegoers."
– Tom Buckley, The New York Times

The Matrix (1999)
"It's astonishing that so much money, talent, technical expertise and visual imagination can be put in the service of something so stupid."
- Bob Graham, San Francisco Chronicle

"The real soullessness here is built into the production, a polished adaptation of Hong Kong-style filmmaking that, with its cast of depressive characters, allows for little Hong Kong-style joy. The Matrix sells itself as a gaudy chopsocky concoction with expensive Hollywood action details - a blast of Holly-Kong glitz that never approaches the stylistic cohesiveness of, say, John Woo's Face/Off or the charisma of that film's propulsive star John Travolta."
- Lisa Schwarzbaum, Entertainment Weekly

Michael Clayton (2007)
"Ultimately wearying." – Jan Stuart, Newsday

Midnight Run (1988)
"The film is too routinely formulaic to be anything more than modestly diverting. Carrying the dead weight of George Gallo's script, Brest isn't up to the strenuous task of transforming his uninspired genre material in something deeper, and so the attempts to mix pathos with comedy strike us merely as wild and disorienting vacillations in tone."
- Hal Hinson, Washington Post

Miller's Crossing (1990)
"Weightless. It is also, unfortunately, without much point at all... A movie of random effects and little accumulative impact."
- Vincent Canby, The New York Times

"A lifeless, tedious picture... A complete dud."
- Stanley Kauffmann, The New Republic

Moonstruck (1987) Best Original Screenplay
"The title refers to one relative's theory that the full moon can make people wildly romantic, make them behave in wonderful, unpredictably crazy ways.
Not crazy enough."
– Janet Maslin, The New York Times

Network (1976) Best Original Screenplay
"The plot that Paddy Chayefsky has concocted to prove this point is so crazily preposterous that even in post-Watergate America -- where we know that bats can get loose in the corridors of power -- it is just impossible to accept."
– Richard Schickel, TIME Magazine

Office Space (1999)

*"Office Space is an expansion of three animated shorts created by Mr. Judge for television over the last decade, and it has the loose-jointed feel of a bunch of sketches packed together into a narrative that doesn't gather much momentum.
Its conspiratorial eager beavers are so undeveloped that they could hardly even be called types. You don't care for a second what happens to them."*
- Stephen Holden, The New York Times

"Drably shot, unimaginatively written and shallowly acted. Take this movie and shove it."
- Chicago Tribune

An Officer and a Gentleman (1982)

"Macho, materialistic, and pro-militarist, it's an objectionable little number made all the more insidious by the way Hackford pulls the strings and turns it into a heart-chilling weepie."
- Time Out London

One Flew Over The Cukoo's Nest (1975)

Best Picture/Director/Actor/Actress

*"I suspect that we are meant to make connections between Randle's confrontation with the oppressive Nurse Ratched and the political turmoil in this country in the 1960's. The connection doesn't work. All it does is conveniently distract us from questioning the accuracy of the film's picture of life in a mental institution where shock treatments are dispensed like aspirins and lobotomies are prescribed as if the mind's frontal lobes were troublesome wisdom teeth.
Even granting the artist his license, America is much too big and various to be satisfactorily reduced to the dimensions of one mental ward in a movie like this."*
- Vincent Canby, The New York Times

"It's a lot easier to make noble points about fighting the establishment, about refusing to surrender yourself to the system, than it is to closely observe the ways real people behave when they're placed in an environment like a mental institution."
– Roger Ebert

Ordinary People (1980)

Best Picture/Director/Adapted Screenplay/Supporting Actor

*"Very much a melodrama of the '80s, following the example of Kramer vs. Kramer by balancing emotional goo with bleached, sterile visuals.
The film looks austere and serious, rather as if it had been shot inside a Frigidaire, and the oppressiveness of the images tends to strangle laughter, even at the most absurd excesses of Alvin Sargent's script. The material, from Judith Guest's novel, mixes family drama with pop-psychological insights, a marriage of Eugene O'Neill and Wayne Dyer. As the tortured son, Tim Hutton steals shamelessly from Tony Perkins's repertoire of twitches and hesitations; if I were Perkins, I would have sued. Mary Tyler Moore shows her wrinkles and nothing else as the mother; Donald Sutherland, as dad, is pink and babyish."*
– Dave Kehr, Chicago Reader

Paper Moon (1973)
"It is very fussy about period detail, and goes to some length to evoke the dim days of Depression America, while just about everything else is left to slide."
- Jay Cocks, TIME Magazine

"Paper Moon is oddly depressing instead of what is usually called heart-warming."
- Vincent Canby, The New York Times

Pee Wee's Big Adventure (1985)
"There are two funny things in Pee-Wee's Big Adventure. One is a waitress who explains why her boyfriend doesn't want to go to Paris. 'He flunked French in high school and now thinks everybody over there is out to make him look dumb.' The other is a pretty, unstoppably gushy young woman (Jan Hooks) who acts as a tour guide at the Alamo in San Antonio. I reveal this information as a consumer service, for Pee-Wee's Big Adventure is otherwise the most barren comedy I've seen in years, maybe ever."
- Vincent Canby, The New York Times

"Fair warning: this movie could induce terminal boredom in adults and rot the minds of the young.
- TIME Magazine

Platoon (1986) Best Picture/Director
"The artistic veneer Stone applies, along with the simpy narration provided for Sheen in the way of letters to his grandmother, detract significantly from the work's immediacy."
– Todd McCarthy, Variety

"I know that Platoon is being acclaimed for its realism, and I expect to be chastened for being a woman finding fault with a war film. But I've probably seen as much combat as most of the men saying, 'This is how war is.'"
– Pauline Kael

Pretty Woman (1990)
"Nothing works, except perhaps the sight of Julia Roberts' lean, well-tempered midsection and her roughly eight yards of legs that, in this frail comedy, are worked until they're almost a story point of their own."
– Sheila Benson, The Los Angeles Times

The Princess Bride (1987)
"Based on William Goldman's novel, this is a post-modern fairy tale that challenges and affirms the conventions of a genre that may not be flexible enough to support such horseplay. It also doesn't help that Cary Elwes and Robin Wright as the loving couple are nearly comatose and inspire little passion from each other, or the audience."
– Variety

"A fairytale as told to a bedridden boy: the willowy Buttercup (Wright) is abducted and whisked through a series of life-threatening exploits and miscast comic cameos. The tone falls disconcertingly between straight action adventure and anachronistic Jewish spoof; the leads are vacuous; the absurdities sometimes forced and obvious."
– Time Out London

Psycho (1960)
"The experienced Hitchcock fan might reasonably expect the unreasonable. What is offered instead is merely gruesome. Little should be said of the plot, director Hitchcock bears down too heavily in this one, and the delicate illusion of reality becomes, instead, a spectacle of stomach-churning horror."
- TIME Magazine

Pulp Fiction (1994) Best Original Screenplay
"Pulp Fiction's anthology of stories about gangster fun and games in Los Angeles doesn't merit sustained veneration. Because Pulp Fiction is sporadically effective, the temptation to embrace the entire two hours and 29 minutes of Tarantiniana is strong.
But in truth this is a noticeably uneven film, both too inward-looking and self-centered in its concerns and too outward-bound in the way it strains to outrage an audience, to be successful across the board. Some sequences, especially one involving bondage harnesses and homosexual rape, have the uncomfortable feeling of creative desperation, of someone who is afraid of losing his reputation scrambling for any way to offend sensibilities."
- Kenneth Turan, Los Angeles Times

Raging Bull (1980) Best Actor
"Robert De Niro is one of the most repugnant and unlikeable screen protagonists in some time. The director excels at whipping up an emotional storm, but seems unaware that there is any need for quieter, more introspective scenes in drama.
The scenes it does choose to show are almost perversely chosen to alienate the audience."
- Joseph McBride, Variety

"What DeNiro does in this picture isn't acting, exactly. I'm not sure what it is. DeNiro seems to have emptied himself out to become the part he's playing and then not got enough material to refill himself with; his LaMotta is a swollen puppet with only bits and pieces of a character inside, and some religious, semi-abstract concepts of guilt."
– Pauline Kael

Raiders Of The Lost Ark (1981)
"Raiders is a machine-tooled adventure in the pulp-esoterica spirit of Edgar Rice Burroughs; it appears that Lucas and Spielberg think just like the marketing division. But Spielberg's technique may be too much for the genre: the opening sequence, set in South America, with Indy Jones entering a forbidden temple and fending off traps, snares, poisoned darts, tarantulas, stone doors with metal teeth, and the biggest damn boulder you've ever seen, is so thrill-packed you don't have time to breathe—or to enjoy yourself much, either.

You know that Spielberg, having gone sky-high at the start, must have at least seventeen other climaxes to come, and that the movie isn't going to be an adventure but a competition. There's no exhilaration in this dumb, motor excitement. Yet, with the manicured wide-screen images and the scale of this production, klunkiness sticks out in a way that it didn't in the serials. The actors are mostly just bodies carrying pieces of plot around.
Raiders is timid moviemaking: the film seems terrified of not giving audiences enough thrills to keep them happy. The whole collapsing industry is being inspired by old Saturday-afternoon serials and the three biggest American moviemakers are hooked on technological playthings and techniques. Seeing Raiders is like being put through a Cuisinart—something has been done to us, but not to our benefit."
- Pauline Kael, The New Yorker

"*I don't myself find that a host of snakes will restore drama to a sagging thriller, but I must tell you that I've never seen a more determined attempt to do so. Serpentine central casting must have been worked to a frazzle. After the escape from entombment and the cobras and asps, the film is simply a bore. So save your money.*"
- Christopher Hitchens, New Statesman

Raising Arizona (1987)
"It often doesn't hold together as a coherent story."
- Variety

"Everyone in Raising Arizona talks funny. They all elevate their dialogue to an arch and artificial level that's distracting and unconvincing and slows down the progress of the film. And what Raising Arizona needs more than anything else is more velocity. Here's a movie that stretches out every moment for more than it's worth, until even the moments of inspiration seem forced.
Since the basic idea is a good one and there are talented people in the cast, what we have here is a film shot down by its own forced and mannered style."
- Roger Ebert, Chicago Sun-Times

Reservoir Dogs (1992)
"Less than the sum of its outrageous gags and inventive bits of business. The story is impressively bloody, but the blood is thin, and it keeps leaking out; Tarantino has all he can do to maintain the movie's pulse. Mostly, he tries to get by on film-school cleverness – a homemade pharmaceutical cocktail of allusions, pop music, and visual jolts."
- Terrence Rafferty, The New Yorker

"I felt sickened by the coldness of this picture's visual cruelty."
- Julie Salamon, The Wall Street Journal

Risky Business (1983)
"Another stupid sex comedy."
– Christian Science Monitor

*"Joel's suburban parents are crude caricatures and a few of his friends
are terrifically unappealing, speaking too slowly and savoring every nuance
of some less than fascinating dialogue."*
– Janet Maslin, The New York Times

Rocky (1976) Best Picture/Best Director
*"Preposterous. One can really not deal with such a howler and at the same time interest
oneself fully with Rocky's quest for a moral victory.
An entire film devoted to so dreary a fellow would be intolerable."*
- Richard Corliss, TIME Magazine

*"Avildsen has an instinct for making serious emotions look tawdry.
He'll go for a cheap touch whenever he can [and] tries to falsify material that was suspect
from the beginning. Even by the standards of fairy tales, it strains logic... stupid song with
couplets like 'feeling strong now/won't be long now."*
– Frank Rich, NY Post

*"The screenplay of Rocky is purest Hollywood make-believe of the 1930's, but there would be
nothing wrong with that, had the film been executed with any verve. Mr. Stallone's Rocky is
less a performance than an impersonation. It's all superficial mannerisms and movements,
reminding me of Rodney Dangerfield doing a nightclub monologue.
The speech patterns sound right, and what he says is occasionally lifelike,
but it's a studied routine, not a character. Most of the film was photographed on location in
seedy, Philadelphia neighborhoods, and it's one of the film's ironies that a production that
has put such emphasis on realism should seem so fraudulent.
Throughout the movie we are asked to believe that his Rocky is compassionate, interesting,
even heroic, though the character we see is simply an unconvincing actor imitating a lug."*
- Vincent Canby, The New York Times

*"A great movie? Hardly. Stallone as the next Brando? You've got to be kidding.
A nice little fantasy picture? Maybe.
That's the hype and reality of Rocky, the flat out schmaltzy saga of a Philadelphia club boxer
who, on New Year's Day of our Bicentennial Year, gets a chance to fight for the heavyweight
championship of the world.
Sylvester Stallone, as likable as a basset hound, stars as Rocky Balboa,
a fighter who, all together now, could've been a contender."*
- Gene Siskel Chicago Tribune

Roger & Me (1989)
*"I've heard it said that Michael Moore's muckraking documentary Roger & Me
is scathing and Voltairean. I've read that Michael Moore is 'a satirist of the Reagan period
equal in talent to Mencken and Lewis,' and 'an irrepressible new humorist in the tradition of
Mark Twain and Artemus Ward.' But the film I saw was shallow and facetious,
a piece of gonzo demagoguery that made me feel cheap for laughing."*
- Pauline Kael

The Royal Tenenbaums (2002)
*"Inappropriate directness informs every second of The Royal Tenenbaums,
and it just about wrecks the movie."*
- CNN

Rushmore (1998)
*"Wes Anderson has an idiosyncratic sensibility,
the rare ability to create a world that is completely his own.
Unique worlds, however, can be off-putting enough to discourage civilians from spending
time there. And that is the case with Rushmore as well."*
– Kenneth Turan, Los Angeles Times

Saving Private Ryan (1998) Best Director
*"The film remains an utterly American take on WWII,
with the lack of political, ethical and historical perspective which that implies.
Why did Spielberg make it? He wants us to imagine we can feel the terror of being there, but
does that make us any wiser about this or any other conflict?
Probably not."*
– Time Out London

"I found it tediously manipulative."
- Andrew Sarris, The New York Observer

Say Anything (1989)
*"A half-baked love story, full of good intentions but uneven in the telling.
Pic also has considerable structural problems, as many scenes feel unachieved."*
- Variety

The Searchers (1956)
*"The Searchers is somewhat disappointing. There is a feeling that it could have been so
much more. Overlong and repetitious at 119 minutes, there are subtleties in the basically
simple story that are not adequately explained. Wayne is a bitter, taciturn individual
throughout and the reasons for his attitude are left to the imagination of the viewer.
The John Ford directorial stamp is unmistakable.
It concentrates on the characters and establishes a definite mood.
It's not sufficient, however, to overcome many of the weaknesses of the story."*
- Ronald Holloway, Variety

Sexy Beast (2000)
*"Sexy Beast has been getting great reviews. Allow me to impose a brief reality check:
It may be almost not bad, if you can understand it, which I couldn't."*
- Stephen Hunter, The Washington Post

The Shawshank Redemption (1994)
"The movie seems to last about half a life sentence and becomes incarcerated in its own labyrinthine sentimentality. And leave it to pandering, first-time director Frank Darabont to ensure no audience member leaves this film unsure of the ending. Heaven forbid a movie should end with a smidgen of mystery!"
- Desson Howe, The Washington Post

The Shining (1980)
"If you go to this adaptation of Stephen King's novel expecting to see a horror movie, you'll be disappointed. The setting is promising enough – an empty, isolated hotel in dead-of-winter Colorado – but Kubrick makes it warm, well-lit and devoid of threat."
- Time Out London

The Silence of the Lambs (1991)
Best Picture/Director/Actor/Actress/Adapted Screenplay
"Has been billed as one of the most frightening, depraved films ever made. Would that it were so. Instead, this is a case of much ado about nothing. Foster's character, who is appealing, is dwarfed by the monsters she is after. I'd rather see her work on another case."
– Gene Siskel, Chicago Tribune

"It's always puzzling when a good director makes a bad movie, but the case of Jonathan Demme's The Silence of the Lambs seems downright baffling. More than a disappointment, the film is an almost systematic denial of Demme's credentials as an artist and filmmaker. This isn't the Jonathan Demme we know."
- Dave Kehr, Chicago Tribune

The Sixth Sense (1999)
"And this year's Touched by an Angel award for gaggingly mawkish supernatural kitsch goes to Bruce Willis's newest film, The Sixth Sense. The star also earns the Robin Williams-manque award for ineffable, twinkling, half-smiling misty-eyed empathy with adorable tots. Because it unfolds like a garish hybrid of Simon Birch and What Dreams May Come, with some horror-movie touches thrown in to keep us from nodding off, The Sixth Sense appears to have been concocted at exactly the moment Hollywood was betting on supernatural schmaltz."
- Stephen Holden, The New York Times

"Despite being an inflated, polished-to-an-anonymous-shine Disney deal, M. Night Shyamalan's The Sixth Sense has its nervous thumb on something. Too bad it ends up being a play date in the Ghost neighborhood. We see only a few genuinely chilling ghosts; mostly, the film feels huddled in apprehension."
– The Village Voice

Sixteen Candles (1984)
"Hughes invokes the classical unities of time, place, and plot symmetry, yet he trashes his careful structure every time he needs a gag - destroying the integrity of his characters, shattering the plausibility of his situations."
– Dave Kehr, Chicago Reader

The Sound Of Music (1965) Best Picture/Director
"The septet of blond and beaming youngsters who have to act like so many Shirley Temples and Freddie Bartholomews when they were young do as well as could be expected with their assortedly artificial roles, but the adults are fairly horrendous."
- Bosley Crowther, The New York Times

Star Wars (1977)
"None of these characters has any depth, and they're all treated like the fanciful props and settings!"
– Jonathan Rosenbaum, Chicago Reader

"There's no breather in the picture, no lyricism; the only attempt at beauty is in the double sunset. It's enjoyable on its own terms, but it's exhausting, too: like taking a pack of kids to the circus. An hour into it, children say that they're ready to see it again; that's because it's an assemblage of spare parts—it has no emotional grip."
– Pauline Kael

"About the dialogue there's nothing to be said. In fact the dialogue itself can hardly be said: it sticks in the actors' mouths like peanut butter. The acting is the School of Buster Crabbe, except for Alec Guinness, who mumbles through on the way to his salary check. The only way that Star Wars could have been exciting was through its visual imagination and special effects. Both are unexceptional."
– Stanley Kauffman, New Republic

"O dull new world! It is all as exciting as last year's weather reports. It is all trite characters and paltry verbiage, handled adequately by Harrison Ford as a blockade-running starship pilot, uninspiredly by Mark Hamill as Luke Skywalker and wretchedly by Carrie Fisher, who is not even appealing as Princess Leia. Sir Alec has a wistful yet weighty dignity of tone and aspect that is all his own; why he should waste it on the likes of Luke, whom he befriends, protects, and bequeaths the Force to, remains the film's one mystery."
– John Simon, New York Magazine

Straw Dogs (1971)
"A major disappointment."
– Roger Ebert, Chicago Sun-Times

Stripes (1981)
"Stripes will keep potential felons off the streets for two hours. Few people seem to be asking, these days, that movies do more."
–TIME Magazine

Taxi Driver (1976)
"[Scorsese] seems to need scripts with well-designed humor and performers with the spirit of Ellen Burstyn to compensate for what seems to be a fundamentally depressed view of life and the belief that sobriety is the equivalent of seriousness."
- Richard Schickel, TIME Magazine

"Remove the cataclysmic ending from Taxi Driver and it would be one smashingly good motion picture. As it stands, the film is beautiful to look at, exciting to listen to, but much too much to stomach."
- Gene Siskel, Chicago Tribune

Terms Of Endearment (1983)
Best Picture/Director/Actress/Adapted Screenplay
"Widowed Houston housewife Shirley MacLaine dominates her implausibly well adjusted, extroverted daughter, Debra Winger; the revenge—unstated and indirect, as popular filmmaking warrants—consists of the daughter presiding over the mother's sexual initiation (via over-the-hill astronaut Jack Nicholson) and a tear-jerking ending that would make Freud cringe. Writer-director James L. Brooks was one of the architects of the MTM sitcom style, and he has television in his soul: his people are incredibly tiny (most are defined by a single stroke of obsessive behavior), and he chokes out his narrative in ten-minute chunks, separated by aching lacunae. The dual-track plot, with constant cutting between mother and daughter, seems less an attempt to establish meaningful parallels between the two stories than the nervous twitches of a compulsive channel changer."
- Dave Kehr, Chicago Reader

There will Be Blood (2007)
"No! is the first word spoken and it should be the last said in response to Paul Thomas Anderson's latest pretend epic."
– Armond White, New York Press

"I hate the way the film forces us into its epic structure and purposely fractured narrative as if the audience is a puppy having its little nose shoved into a puddle of its own making."
– Donald Munro, The Fresno Bee

This Is Spinal Tap (1984)
"The attitudes are too narrow to nourish a feature-length film."
- Dave Kehr, Chicago Reader

Titanic (1997) Best Picture/Director
"Cost well over $200m. Disregarding the ethics of such expenditure on a film, this unprecedented extravagance has not resulted in sophisticated or even very satisfying storytelling."
– Time Out, London

"What audiences end up with word-wise is a hackneyed, completely derivative copy of old Hollywood romances, a movie that reeks of phoniness and lacks even minimal originality."
- Kenneth Turan, Los Angeles Times

"The regretful verdict here: dead in the water."
- Richard Corliss, TIME Magazine

Trading Places (1983)
"Rich boy and poor boy swap lives.
The only reason for using a plotline as primitive as this is to give two improvisational comics like Dan Aykroyd and Eddie Murphy plenty of room to maneuver.
But director John Landis is so deficient in basic storytelling skills that he must spend hours explicating the most elementary plot points while Aykroyd and Murphy are sidelined."
- Dave Kehr, Chicago Reader

The Treasure of the Sierra Madre (1948)
"It should be finally remarked that women have small place in this picture, which is just one more reason why it is good."
– Bosley Crowther, The New York Times

2001: A Space Odyssey (1968)
"2001 lacks dramatic appeal to a large degree and only conveys suspense after the halfway mark. The plot, so-called, uses up almost two hours in exposition of scientific advances in space travel and communications, before anything happens, [including] the surprisingly dull prolog. The film ends on a confused note, never really tackling the 'other life' situation and evidently leaving interpretation up to the individual viewer.
To many this will smack of indecision or hasty scripting."
- Robert B. Frederick, Variety

Unforgiven (1992) Best Picture/Director
"By now, Eastwood has little more than a paint-by-numbers approach to acting. As a result, we relate to Munny more as a compendium of Eastwood's earlier characters."
- Hal Hinson, The Washington Post

"While Eastwood dedicates the film to Sergio Leone and Don Siegel, his early directors, he doesn't seem to have learned all that much from them.
If their action films had been this plodding, nobody would ever have heard of Clint Eastwood outside of television's Rawhide."
– People Magazine

Waiting For Guffman (1996)
"Outside the fest circuit, Waiting for Guffman seems a candidate for cable and homevid rather than theatrical release."
- Variety

Wet Hot American Summer (2001)
"I want to escape, / Oh, Muddah Faddah-- / Life's too short for cinematic torture."
– Roger Ebert, Chicago Sun-Times

"This is supposed to be funny? It was so depressing I almost started to cry."
- Stephen Hunter, Washington Post

West Side Story (1961) 9 Oscar's® including Best Picture
"Unhappily, the film shares a serious flaw in the essential conception of the show; both are founded on a phony literary analogy and on some potentially vicious pseudo-sociology."
—TIME Magazine

What About Bob? (1991)
"A sentimental comedy about mental illness (complete with a sitcom family), wobbly Bob offers further evidence that Disney itself may be afflicted with encroaching schizophrenia."
- Mike Clark, USA Today

"It's a bomb - not the usual bomb, but a time bomb..."
- Mick LaSalle, San Francisco Chronicle

Witness (1985)
"Weir, an Australian filming in this country for the first time has succumbed to blandness."
– Pauline Kael, The New Yorker

"It's not really awful, but it's not much fun."
- Vincent Canby, The New York Times

Battlefield Earth (2000)
"Is it worth seeing once? Sure."
- Bob Graham, San Francisco Chronicle

Batman and Robin (1997)
"A wild, campy costume party of a movie."
- Janet Maslin, The New York Times

Catwoman (2004)
"Catwoman is as swift and light on its feet as its heroine, Halle Berry."
– Kevin Thomas, Los Angeles Times

*"Catwoman has a dark elegance and stylish moves.
It's an odd, idiosyncratic movie -- dark in look and dark in spirit –
that plays as a kind of pop culture investigation into the meaning of feminism and the options open to women in the modern world.
I think when the future weighs in on Catwoman, it will decide that its unintended message is that independence is great, so long as women don't take it too far.
But in the meantime, there's Friday night, and for Friday night this will do just fine."*
- Mick LaSalle, San Francisco Chronicle

Eat, Pray, Love (2010)
"The movie is aware of its own riches; it fills up your plate and dares you not to eat."
- Time Out London

Firewall (2006)
"It kept me alert, terrified and royally entertained."
- Rex Reed, New York Observer

Garfield: A Tail of Two Kitties (2006)
"Good kitty! Superior in every way to its underwhelming predecessor, Garfield: A Tail of Two Kitties is a genuinely clever kidpic that should delight moppets, please parents — and maybe tickle a few tweens."
– Joe Leydon, Variety

Ghostbusters 2 (1989)
"Even the special effects are more to the point of the comedy than they were in the first film. For some reason, this appears to leave more room for the sort of random funny business that Mr. Murray and his friends do best."
-Vincent Canby, The New York Times

Gigli (2003)
"An enjoyably written and performed romantic comedy."
- Amy Dawes, Variety

The Godfather: Part III (1991)
"Andy Garcia, who first became noticeable in The Untouchables, has seductive strength, homicidal cool. One reason to look forward to Part IV is that he'll fill the center better than Pacino does."
– Stanley Kauffmann, The New Republic

Grown-Ups (2010)
"Sandler's reckless comedy pokes fun at his clique's immaturity. He doesn't pretend to create character studies; rather, he satirizes their common silliness as they revisit adolescent pranks and attitudes. One ploy of Sandler and Fred Wolf's screenplay is to democratize humor—spread affectionate derision all around—by repeating jokes that grow into an appreciation of our full humanity. Unassuming as it is, Grown Ups' best moments suggest a humanist work of art."
- Armond White, New York Press

Hannibal (2001)
"This superior sequel has romance in its dark heart."
- Richard Corliss, TIME Magazine

The Happening (2008)
"Shyamalan's approach is more effective than smash-and-grab plot-mongering. His use of the landscape is disturbingly effective. The performances by Wahlberg and Deschanel bring a quiet dignity to their characters."
-Roger Ebert, Chicago Sun-Times

I Now Pronounce You Chuck & Larry (2007)
"It's a modern classic. By comparison, Hollywood's most celebrated gay comedies -- In and Out, Chuck and Buck, Blades of Glory, even the laughable Brokeback Mountain – were all failures of nerve."
- Armond White, New York Press

Ishtar (1987)
"Ishtar is a good movie, but you can't help but wonder if, lurking somewhere in those cans of outtakes, there isn't a great movie, too."
– Dave Kehr, Chicago Tribune

"A smart, generous, genuinely funny affair. Sometimes, like the camel who almost ambles away with the picture, it's longish in the tooth, but it is based on an extremely astute vision of life."
- Sheila Benson, Los Angeles Times

Jack and Jill (2011)
"Adam Sandler, the least abashed comic actor outside the Borscht Belt, tackles Jewish self-deprecation in this sibling rivalry laff fest. Playing both male and female twins, Sandler shows tribal affection by turning bad vibes into good. Al Pacino's cameo as Jill's suitor is both crazily romantic and a brilliant professional salute."
– Armond White, New York Press

Pearl Harbor (2001)
"For my money a much better heartbreaker, thrillmaker and tear-tweaker than Titanic."
- Stephen Hunter, Washington Post

Showgirls (1992)
"Who knew such a seamy swim in the misogynistic swill of life could be so entertaining?"
- Susan Wloszczyna, USA Today

Speed 2 – Cruise Control (1997)
"Is the movie fun? Yes. Movies like this embrace goofiness with an almost sensual pleasure. And so, on a warm summer evening, do I."
- Roger Ebert, Chicago Sun-Times

"Our Flick of the Week succeeds just as its predecessor did by giving us enough fresh action for two movies, hosted by two extremely attractive performers. Speed 2 is the most exciting to date of this summer's big action pictures."
-Gene Siskel, Chicago Tribune

Star Wars: Episode II - Attack of the Clones (2002)
"An exhilarating two hours of serious fun."
- Richard Corliss, TIME Magazine

That's My Boy (2012)
"The basic joke keeps on giving and the sweetness of the parent-child bonding scenes plays well."
- Time Out London

Transformers: Revenge Of The Fallen (2009)
"With machines that are impressively more lifelike, and characters that are more and more like machines, Transformers: Revenge of the Fallen takes the franchise to a vastly superior level of artificial intelligence."
- Jordan Mintzer, Variety

PRO TIPS

*"If you're not failing every now and again,
it's a sign you're not doing anything very innovative."*
- Woody Allen

"There are no rules in filmmaking. Only sins. And the cardinal sin is dullness."
- Frank Capra

*"I don't want to be a part of the demographics. I want to be an individual.
I wear each of my films as a badge of pride. That's why I cherish all my bad reviews.
If the critics start liking my movies, then I'm in deep trouble."*
- John Carpenter

*"You're just poor cornball provincial people, you critics;
you just don't know what the hell you're talking about."*
- George Cukor

*"As for critics, one mediocre writer is more valuable than ten good critics.
They are like haughty, barren spinsters lodged in a maternity ward."*
- Peter Greenaway

*"We have gotten some terrible reviews at times but if we depended on the judgment of the
studios or critics, we never would have made more than one movie."*
- Ismail Merchant

"Pain is temporary, film is forever!"
- John Milius

*"A lot of critics sometimes get into analyzing the way actors direct
versus non-actors directing. And they really always miss it.
It's one of those things where, by not being practitioners,
they just came up with something that made sense to them."*
- Sean Penn

*"You know, if I started worrying about what the critics think, I'd never make another
comedy. You couldn't pick a less funny group than critics
- you couldn't find a more bitter group of people."*
- Todd Phillips, Director of The Hangover.

"Some day I'll make a film that critics will like. When I have money to waste."
- Francois Truffaut

"The only pictures worth making are the ones that are playing with fire."
- Billy Wilder

BAD CALLS

"The cinema is little more than a fad. It's canned drama. What audiences really want to see is flesh and blood on the stage."
- Charlie Chaplin (1916).

"The idea will never work, a giant mouse on the screen will terrify women."
– MGM rejection for Mickey Mouse (1927).

"Who the hell wants to hear actors talk?"
–H.M. Warner, Warner Brothers re; "talkies" (1927).

"His ears are too big and he looks like an ape."
- Darryl F. Zanuck rejecting Clark Gable for *Little Caesar* (1931).

"Gone With the Wind is going to be the biggest flop in Hollywood history. I'm glad it'll be Clark Gable who's falling flat on his face, not me."
–Gary Cooper on his decision not to take the leading role.

"The song is no good. It isn't a hit."
- *An Officer and a Gentleman* producer Don Simpson demanding *"Up Where We Belong"* be cut from the film.
The song became a #1 hit, winning an Oscar® and a Grammy.

"A wimpy Walt Disney movie."
– Columbia Pictures, passing on *E.T.: The Extra-Terrestrial*.

"Too demented."
– TriStar Chairman Mike Medavoy, rejecting *Pulp Fiction*.

"This is the worst thing ever written. It makes no sense. Someone's dead and then they're alive? It's too long, violent, and un-filmable."
– Columbia/TriStar executive, also turning down *Pulp Fiction*.

Essanay

Your manuscript is returned for the reason checked below:

1. OVERSTOCKED.
2. NO STRONG DRAMATIC SITUATIONS.
3. WEAK PLOT.
4. NOT OUR STYLE OF STORY.
5. IDEA HAS BEEN DONE BEFORE. ✓
6. WOULD NOT PASS THE CENSOR BOARD.
7. TOO DIFFICULT TO PRODUCE.
8. TOO CONVENTIONAL.
9. NOT INTERESTING.
10. NOT HUMOROUS.
11. NOT ORIGINAL.
12. NOT ENOUGH ACTION.
13. NO ADAPTATIONS DESIRED.
14. IMPROBABLE.
15. NO COSTUME PLAYS, OR STORIES WITH FOREIGN SETTINGS DESIRED.
16. ILLEGIBLE.
17. ROBBERY, KIDNAPPING, MURDER, SUICIDE, HARROWING DEATH-BED AND ALL SCENES OF AN UNPLEASANT NATURE SHOULD BE ELIMINATED.

Yours very truly,
ESSANAY FILM MFG. CO.,

Studio and Laboratories
1333 Argyle St.

CHICAGO, ILL.

MAVERICKS

"If you're going through hell, keep going."
- Winston Churchill

Winston Churchill (1874-1965)
"Never, never, in nothing great or small, large or petty, never give in except to convictions of honour and good sense. Never yield to force; never yield to the apparently overwhelming might of the enemy."

Throughout his life Churchill suffered from clinical depression,
which he called his "black dog".
As a child, he struggled in school, was raised mostly by a nanny and had
a terrible speech impediment.
It took him three tries to pass the exam for Military College.
In 1899, Churchill left the army to go to work as a war correspondent.
While reporting on the Boer War, he was taken prisoner and soon escaped,
traveling 300 miles to safety. Instead of returning home, he rejoined the army and
remained on active duty until retiring in 1924, at the age of fifty.
In 1939, Churchill fiercely criticized Prime Minister Neville Chamberlain's appeasement
of Hitler and in a speech to the House of Commons, said:
*"You were given the choice between war and dishonor.
You chose dishonor, and you will have war."*
On May 10, 1940, Churchill was appointed Prime Minister.
He was 65 years old, the age when most people retire.
Hours later, Germany invaded France.
On June 4, 1940, when Britain alone stood against Hitler in Europe,
Churchill spoke to Parliament's House of Commons:

*"We shall go on to the end, we shall fight in France, we shall fight on the seas and oceans, we shall fight with growing confidence and growing strength in the air,
we shall defend our island, whatever the cost may be, we shall fight on the beaches,
we shall fight on the landing grounds, we shall fight in the fields and in the streets,
we shall fight in the hills; we shall never surrender."*

Churchill led Britain from the edge of defeat,
until victory over Nazi Germany had been secured.
He is now widely regarded as one of the greatest wartime leaders in history.

Charles Darwin (1809-1882)
*"I was considered by all my masters and my father, a very ordinary boy,
rather below the common standard of intellect."*
Darwin was often criticized by his father for being lazy and too dreamy.
He later published *On the Origin of Species* in 1859, saying:
*"I see no good reasons why the views given in this volume
should shock the religious sensibilities of anyone."*
Evolution was met with outrage from many who believed in creationism.
Darwin became known as one of the most influential figures in human history.
An overwhelming majority of the worldwide scientific community and
the educated public now accepts evolution as a fact.

Thomas Edison (1847-1931)
"Too stupid to learn anything." - One of Edison's teachers.
He was later fired from jobs for *"not being productive enough."*
When working at Western Union in 1867, he used his time to conduct experiments. One night he spilled battery acid, which ate through the floorboards. He was fired.
Many of his early attempts failed, but he persevered, saying:
"If I find 10,000 ways something won't work, I haven't failed. I am not discouraged, because every wrong attempt discarded is another step forward."
He later invented the stock ticker, the phonograph, the motion picture camera and the first practical light bulb.
"Many of life's failures are people who did not realize how close they were to success when they gave up."

Albert Einstein (1879-1955)
"Great spirits have always encountered violent opposition from mediocre minds."
As a child, Einstein's father intended for him to become an electrical engineer but he clashed with authorities and resented traditional teaching methods. Later writing:
"The spirit of learning and creative thought were lost in strict rote learning."
Einstein failed entrance to the Zurich Polytechnic School
After graduating from The Argovian School, he spent two years trying to land a teaching job before becoming a patent clerk.
In 1903, he was passed over for promotion because he hadn't
"fully mastered machine technology."
Later, Einstein started a small discussion group, jokingly named "The Olympia Academy", which met regularly to discuss science and philosophy.
His theories on science were published
and he was eventually awarded a Nobel Prize in Physics.
He's known today as one of the most intelligent men in history.

Dwight D. Eisenhower (1890-1969)
When Ike was 2 years-old, his family had $24 to their name.
In high-school, he developed a leg infection and his doctor insisted it be amputated. Ike refused to allow it, and recovered.
He and brother both wanted to attend college, but the family lacked the funds.
He ended up at West Point, in part because tuition was free.
As Supreme Allied Commander in World War II, when German forces had surprised and overwhelmed our troops at the start of the Battle of the Bulge,
Ike called a meeting on December 19, 1944 and said:
"The present situation is to be regarded as opportunity for us and not disaster. There will be only cheerful faces at this conference table."
In what proved to be the decisive battle of WWII,
Eisenhower took advantage of a seemingly hopeless situation.
He became a 5-star General and 34th President of The United States.

Robert Goddard (1882-1945)

When Goddard first proposed a liquid fueled rocket,
he was ridiculed by the scientific community, the public and the press.
On January 13, 1920 The New York Times wrote:
*"A Severe Strain on Credulity – That Professor Goddard does not know the relation of action
and reaction, and of the need to have something better than a vacuum
against which to react—to say that would be absurd.
Of course he only seems to lack the knowledge ladled out daily in high schools."*
Goddard responded:
*"Every vision is a joke until the first man accomplishes it;
once realized, it becomes commonplace."*
He launched the first liquid-fueled rocket on March 16, 1926.
In 1969, 50 years after mocking Goddard and the day after Apollo 11 launched,
The N.Y. Times issued a correction:
*"Further investigation and experimentation have confirmed the findings of Isaac Newton in
the 17th Century and it is now definitely established that a rocket can function in a vacuum
as well as in an atmosphere. The Times regrets the error."*

Ulysses S. Grant (1822-1885)

He was 5'1" and weighed 117 pounds when he entered West Point at age 17.
Forced to resign as an army captain because he was drunk while off-duty, his father tried
to have him reinstated because he believed his son had no other prospects.
As a failed farmer in 1859, Grant freed his slave rather than sell him,
although slaves commanded a high price and Grant was broke.
He later worked as a bill collector and a clerk in a tannery. Both ended in failure.
When The Civil War began in 1861, Grant joined the Union Army as a civilian.
He was soon promoted to Colonel and later General.
Grant became a war hero and later, twice elected President.
He was known for his efforts to remove the vestiges of Confederate nationalism and
slavery, protect African-American citizenship, and defeat the Ku Klux Klan.

Martin Luther King, Jr. (1929-1968)

King battled depression throughout his life and tried to commit suicide at the age of 12 by
jumping out of a second story window. While returning home by bus from a high school
debate, King and his teacher were made to stand so that white passengers could sit.
Infuriated, he channeled his energies into effecting change.
As a pastor in 1959, King became interested in Gandhi's pacifism, traveling to India.
*"Since being in India, I am more convinced than ever before that the method of nonviolent
resistance is the most potent weapon available to oppressed people
in their struggle for justice and human dignity".*
A brilliant orator, King advocated non-violent civil disobedience and galvanized the civil
rights movement. He was instrumental in changing the laws of the land.
King became the youngest recipient of the Nobel Peace Prize, was posthumously awarded
the Presidential Medal of Freedom and his birthday is a federal holiday.

Abraham Lincoln (1809-1865)

There are many uplifting tales of Lincoln overcoming adversity such as "entering the war a captain and emerging a Private" and so on, most of which are dubious.

What is known about Lincoln:

Born into a poor farm family, he lost his mother to illness when he was 9-years-old.

He later became a self-educated lawyer.

By all accounts, Lincoln encountered and overcame many difficulties in his life including job losses, profound heartache and numerous political setbacks.

After the death of his first great love, Ann Rutledge in 1935, Lincoln spiraled into a gloomy melancholy, which haunted him for the rest of his life.

On January 23, 1841 he wrote: *"I am now the most miserable man living. If what I feel were equally distributed to the whole human family, there would not be one cheerful face on the earth. Whether I shall ever be better I can not tell; I awfully forebode I shall not. To remain as I am is impossible; I must die or be better, it appears to me."*

Most believe he seriously considered suicide more than once.

By the late 1850's, he channeled his energy into fighting for the abolition of slavery.

His political enemy, Stephen Douglas wished to allow local voters the right to decide for themselves whether slavery was allowed. Lincoln felt slavery was morally wrong and conflicted with the ideals of our country: *"Slavery is founded in the selfishness of man's nature. Opposition to it, is his love of justice."*

The men debated seven times in 1858, ostensibly for a senate campaign, but in reality the future of our nation was at stake. The Lincoln/Douglas debates became the most important political debates in the history of this nation.

Lincoln lost his election for the Senate seat.

On February 27, 1860, he spoke to a gathering at New York's Cooper Union: *"Let us have faith that right makes might, and in that faith, let us, to the end, dare to do our duty as we understand it"*

He was elected President in November.

The Civil War began in 1861, the most significant moral, political and ideological crisis our nation had ever experienced.

In February, 1862 his eleven-year-old son, Willie died.

Lincoln led the United States through The Civil War, abolishing slavery and preserving the foundations of freedom. On April 9, 1865 the Civil War ended.

Less than a week later, he was assassinated.

He persevered through crushing defeats, heartache, loss and deep depression because he felt he had a higher purpose.

Lincoln is considered one of the greatest U.S. President's ever.

Nelson Mandela (1918-2013)

"I am the master of my fate: I am the captain of my soul."

- From *Invictus*, written on a scrap of paper in his jail cell.

After being imprisoned for 27 years for his belief in equality, Mandela became the first representatively democratic elected President of South Africa.

He later won The Nobel Peace Prize and is often referred to in South Africa as "Tata" meaning "Father of the Nation".

John D. Rockefeller (1839-1937)
"I do not think that there is any other quality so essential to success of any kind as the quality of perseverance."
The son of a con-man, Rockefeller worked his way up from nothing to become the wealthiest person in recorded history.
He spent the last 40 years of his life as a philanthropist.

Theodore Roosevelt (1858-1919)
In 1884, two days after his wife gave birth to their first child,
Roosevelt's mother died. Eleven hours later, his wife died.
He was shattered, writing in his diary: *"The light has gone out of my life."*
He left New York and became a Sheriff in the Dakota Badlands.
When his ranch failed, he returned to New York City to become Police Commissioner, then a war hero, then Governor of New York, Vice-President and eventually, the youngest President in our country's history.
As President, he was a conservationist, designating millions of acres for protection:
"I recognize the right and duty of this generation to develop and use the nature resources of our land; but I do not recognize the right to waste them, or to rob, by wasteful use, the generations that come after us."
In 1912, en route to give a speech, he survived an assassination attempt.
He gave the speech with a bullet lodged in his chest before going to the hospital.
Roosevelt later won the Nobel Peace Prize.

Socrates (470 BC-399 BC)
Socrates radical philosophies and questioning of the prevailing notions of *"might makes right"* humiliated Athenian leaders and led to his being put on trial.
When asked to propose his own punishment,
he suggested a wage paid by the government and free dinners forever.
He was found guilty of *"immoral corrupting of youth"* and sentenced to death.
He's now known as one of the greatest philosophers of the era.

Wilbur Wright (1867-1912), Orville Wright (1871-1948)
"If we worked on the assumption that what is accepted as true really is true, then there would be little hope for advance."
Orville was expelled from elementary school, neither graduated high school and both struggled with depression. They pursued an interest in creating a flying machine, despite no special skills. In 1903, after years of trial and error, their flying experiment first succeeded. In 1906, reports of their flights were met with skepticism. The Herald Tribune published a headline: *"FLYERS OR LIARS?"*
They contacted the U.S. government, Great Britain, France and Germany with an offer to sell their flying machine but were rebuffed because nobody believed them.
Finally, on August 8, 1908 they held a public demonstration.
The brothers instantly became world famous and all skeptics were silenced.
L'Aérophile wrote: *"[The flights] have completely dissipated all doubts.
Not one of the former detractors of the Wrights dare question, today, the previous experiments of the men who were truly the first to fly."*

PRO TIPS

"Take risks: if you win, you will be happy; if you lose, you will be wise."
– Anonymous

"You yourself, as much as anybody in the entire universe, deserve your love and affection."
- Buddha

"Success is going from failure to failure without loss of enthusiasm."
- Winston Churchill

"Our greatest glory is not in never falling, but in rising every time we fall."
- Confucius

"Hell, there are no rules here – we're trying to accomplish something."
-Thomas Edison

*"Out of clutter, find simplicity. From discord, find harmony.
In the middle of difficulty, lies opportunity"*
- Albert Einstein

"Whatever you do will be insignificant, but it is very important that you do it."
- Mahatma Gandhi

"Only those who dare to fail greatly can achieve greatly."
- Robert F. Kennedy

*"If you can't fly, then run.
If you can't run, then walk.
If you can't walk, then crawl,
but whatever you do,
you have to keep moving forward."*
- Martin Luther King, Jr.

"Once a person is determined to help themselves, there is nothing that can stop them."
- Nelson Mandela

"Do what you can, with what you have, where you are."
- Theodore Roosevelt

"We were lucky enough to grow up in an environment where there was always much encouragement to children to pursue intellectual interests; to investigate what ever aroused curiosity."
- Orville Wright

BAD CALLS

*"Inventions have long since reached their limit,
and I see no hope for further developments."*
- Roman engineer Julius Sextus Frontinus (40-103 AD).

*"So many centuries after the Creation it is unlikely that anyone
could find hitherto unknown lands of any value."*
- Committee Investigating proposal for Expedition by Christopher Columbus (1486).

"Pfft! A woman might piss it out."
- Sir Thomas Bloodworth, Lord Mayor of London,
downplaying what became the Great Fire of London (1666).

"The American colonies have little stomach for revolution."
- King George II (1773).

*"I would sooner believe that two Yankee professors lied,
than that stones fell from the sky."*
- Thomas Jefferson after hearing reports of meteorites (1790s).

*"What, sir, would you make a ship sail against the wind
and currents by lighting a bonfire under her deck?
I pray you, excuse me, I have not the time to listen to such nonsense."*
- Napoleon Bonaparte (c. 1800).

*"What can be more palpably absurd than the prospect held out of locomotives traveling
twice as fast as stagecoaches?"*
- The Quarterly Review (1825).

"Ours has been the first, and doubtless to be the last, to visit this profitless locality."
- Lt. Joseph Ives, after visiting the Grand Canyon (1861).

*"No one will pay good money to get from Berlin to Potsdam in one hour when he can ride his
horse there in one day for free."*
- King William I of Prussia re; the invention of trains (1864).

"Louis Pasteur's theory of germs is ridiculous fiction."
- Pierre Pachet, Professor of Physiology at Toulouse (1872).

*"The abdomen, the chest, and the brain will forever be shut
from the intrusion of the wise and humane surgeon."*
–Sir John Eric Erichsen, British Surgeon-Extraordinary to Queen Victoria (1873).

*"When the Paris Exhibition closes, electric light will close with it
and no more will be heard of it."*
- Oxford University professor Erasmus Wilson (1878).

*"Such startling announcements as these should be deprecated as being unworthy of science
and mischievous to its true progress."*
- Sir William Siemens re; invention of the light bulb (1880).

"We are probably nearing the limit of all we can know about astronomy."
– Astronomer Simon Newcomb (1888).

*"Over the next century Law will be simplified.
Lawyers will have diminished, and their fees will have been vastly curtailed."*
- Junius Henri Browne (1893).

"Heavier-than-air flying machines are impossible."
–Lord Kelvin, President of the Royal Society (1895).

"Fooling around with AC electricity is just a waste of time. Nobody will use it, ever."
- Thomas Edison (1899).

"Radio has no future".
–Lord Kelvin, President of the Royal Society (1899).

"Man will not fly for 50 years."
- Wilbur Wright (1901).

"Sensible and responsible women do not want to vote."
- President Grover Cleveland (1905).

"Airplanes are interesting toys but of no military value."
- Marechal Ferdinand Foch, Professor of Strategy, École
Superieure de Guerre (1911).

"You will be home before the leaves have fallen from the trees."
- Kaiser Wilhelm speaking to the German troops (1914).

"There is no likelihood man can ever tap the power of the atom."
- Robert Millikan Physicist and Nobel Prize winner (1923).

*"There is not the slightest indication that nuclear energy will ever be obtainable. It would
mean that the atom would have to be shattered at will."*
- Albert Einstein (1932).

"By the year 1982 the graduated income tax will have practically abolished major differences in wealth."
- Irwin Edman, Professor Columbia University (1932).

"A rocket will never be able to leave the Earth's atmosphere."
- The New York Times (1936).

"Atomic energy might be as good as our present-day explosives, but it is unlikely to produce anything very much more dangerous."
- Winston Churchill (1939).

"The Americans are good about making fancy cars and refrigerators, but that doesn't mean they are any good at making aircraft. They are bluffing. They are excellent at bluffing."
- Hermann Goering (1942).

"The bomb will never go off. I speak as an expert in explosives."
- Admiral William Leahy, U.S. Atomic Bomb Project (1943).

"If excessive smoking actually plays a role in the production of lung cancer, it seems to be a minor one."
- National Cancer Institute (1954).

"Before man reaches the moon, your mail will be delivered within hours from New York to Australia by guided missiles. We stand on the threshold of rocket mail."
- U.S. Postmaster Arthur Summerfield (1959).

"By 1985, machines will be capable of doing any work man can do."
- Herbert A. Simon, Carnegie Mellon University (1965).

"The time has come to close the book on infectious diseases. We have basically wiped out infection in the United States."
- William Stewart, United States Surgeon General (1967).

"[By the turn of the century], if anything remains more or less unchanged, it will be the role of women."
- Harvard sociologist David Riesman (1967).

"It will be years -- not in my time -- before a woman will become Prime Minister."
- Margaret Thatcher (1969).

"That virus is a pussycat."
- Dr. Peter Duesberg re; HIV (1988).

MUSIC

"Do not fear mistakes - there are none."
- Miles Davis

AC/DC - High Voltage (1975) Debut record
"AC/DC is an Australian hard-rock band whose main purpose on earth apparently is to offend anyone within sight or earshot. They succeed on both counts.
Those concerned with the future of hard rock may take solace in knowing that with the release of the first U.S. album by these Australian gross-out champions,
the genre has unquestionably hit its all-time low.
Stupidity bothers me. Calculated stupidity offends me."
- Billy Altman, Rolling Stone

Adele - 19 (2008) Debut record
"There is scant emotional heft behind Adele's prodigiously rich voice,
little bite to her songwriting."
– The Guardian U.K.

Adele – 21 (2011)
"Three years on from her 19 debut, 21 finds Adele feigning maturity,
though in many cases here that apparently involves a sad capitulation to the kind of dreary ballads and overwrought delivery that does her few favours.
The rest of the album sinks into a mire of turgid, characterless piano balladry swamped in routine string arrangements."
- The Independent U.K.

"Her label has thrown the works at the second album by croak-voiced Brit-School brat Adele. There's no Chasing Pavements style killer, but she has murdered
The Cure's Lovesong using Heart FM-friendly jazz-lite as her weapon."
- The Independent on Sunday U.K.

The B-52's - Wild Planet (1980)
"The group's cutesiness overwhelms its artfulness and eliminates all semblance of real emotion. Besides, nobody here can sing as well as Darlene Love –
or Donna Summer, for that matter."
- Dave Marsh, Rolling Stone

The Beatles (1960-1970)
"Not to mince words, Mr. Epstein, but we don't like your boys' sound.
Groups are out; four-piece groups with guitars particularly are finished."
- Dick Rowe of Decca Records, rejecting The Beatles (1962).

On New Years day in 1962, the unknown and unsigned Beatles performed 15 songs at a live audition for Decca records. Decca rejected them.
They soon signed with EMI, but the bad reviews continued:

"With their bizarre shrubbery, the Beatles are obviously a press agent's dream combo. Not even their mothers would claim that they sing well."
- Los Angeles Times, Feb. 11, 1964.

*"Visually they are a nightmare, tight, dandified Edwardian-Beatnik suits
and great pudding bowls of hair.
Musically they are a near disaster, guitars and drums slamming out a merciless beat that
does away with secondary rhythms, harmony and melody.
Their lyrics (punctuated by nutty shouts of 'yeah, yeah, yeah') are a catastrophe,
a preposterous farrago of Valentine-card romantic sentiments."*
– Newsweek, Feb. 24, 1964.

*"The Beatles are not merely awful;
I would consider it sacrilegious to say anything less than that they are god-awful.
They are so unbelievably horribly, so appallingly unmusical, so dogmatically insensitive to
the magic of the art that they qualify as crowned heads of anti-music."*
- Boston Globe, Sept. 13, 1964.

The Beatles- Sgt. Pepper's Lonely Heart's Club Band (1967)
*"Like an over-attended child, this album is spoiled.
It reeks of horns and harps, harmonica quartets, assorted animal noises,
and a 41-piece orchestra.
The Beatles have given us an album of special effects,
dazzling but ultimately fraudulent."*
- Richard Goldstein, The New York Times

The Beatles - Abbey Road (1969)
"I don't much like it."
- Ed Ward, Rolling Stone

Ludwig van Beethoven (1770-1827) 9th Symphony (1824)
*"We find Beethoven's Ninth Symphony to be precisely one hour and five minutes long;
a frightful period indeed, which puts the muscles and lungs of the band,
and the patience of the audience to a severe trial."*
- The Harmonicon, London (April, 1825)

Beethoven's 9th has become one of the best-known and most highly praised works in all
of classical music.

Georges Bizet (1838-1875) - Carmen (1875)
"I foresee a definite and hopeless flop." – Georges Bizet

*"The characters evoke no interest in the spectators,
nay, more, they are eminently repulsive."*
- Music Trade Review (1878)

"As a work of art, it is naught."
– The New York Times (1878)

"The composer of Carmen is nowhere deep; his passionateness is all on the surface, and the general effect of the work is artificial and insincere."
– Boston Gazette (1879)
Bizet believed Carmen was a failure and died shortly after its debut.
It's now considered one of the greatest operas ever written.

Björk - Debut (1993) Debut record
"Rather than sticking to rock & roll, Debut is painfully eclectic. Producer Nellee Hooper has sabotaged a ferociously iconoclastic talent with a phalanx of cheap electronic gimmickry. Björk's singular skills cry out for genuine band chemistry, and instead she gets Hooper's Euro art-school schlock – and we do, too."
- Tom Graves, Rolling Stone

Black Sabbath - Black Sabbath (1970) Debut record
"Just like Cream, but worse. The whole album is a shuck — despite the murky song titles and some inane lyrics, the album has nothing to do with spiritualism, the occult, or anything much except stiff recitations of Cream clichés that sound like the musicians learned them out of a book, grinding on and on with dogged persistence."
- Lester Bangs, Rolling Stone

Blondie - Parallel Lines (1978)
"Punk's answer to Linda Ronstadt? Blondie's Deborah Harry does for Patti Smith what Alice Cooper did for Iggy Pop: swipes a minor good idea and beats it to death."
- Dave Marsh, Rolling Stone

David Bowie - Diamond Dogs (1974)
"Despite two good songs and some thoughtful (if unhummable) rock sonorities, this is doomsday purveyed from a pleasure dome. Message: eat, snort, and be pervy, for tomorrow we shall be peoploids— but tonight how about buying this piece of plastic? Say nay."
- Robert Christgau

Jackson Browne – Jackson Browne (1972) Debut record
"It's not just the blandness of the music, but of the ideas as well, each reinforcing the other."
– Robert Christgau

Jackson Browne – Late For The Sky (1974)
"Browne reminds me of Nixon: no matter how hard I listen to his pronouncements-- important sociologically if nothing else, right? --my mind begins to wander."
– Robert Christgau

The Carpenters (1969-1983)
"The Carpenters are probably the most important American group currently wafting their brand of sublime pap through mass-Media consciousness, eroding all the rough edges and transforming the listener into a contented zombie. Karen possesses the perfect set of vocal chords - a tone like cut-glass with absolutely no sense of feeling or acknowledgement to human frailty in her delivery."
– Nick Kent, NME

"Singles, a greatest-hits collection, says it all. Bubbly and bland."
- Stephen Holden, Rolling Stone

Enrico Caruso (1873-1921)
"You will never succeed as a singer."
– His first voice coach
Caruso became one of the most revered tenors in history.

Cream - Wheels of Fire (1968)
"Cream is good at a number of things; unfortunately songwriting and recording are not among them."
- Jann Wenner, Rolling Stone

Bob Dylan - Planet Waves (1974)
"Planet Waves sounded hasty, unfinished.
He was once more recording with the Band, something he had not done for a full album, but there simply was not enough good material to produce the sort of major work expected from a performer of Dylan's stature.
The best songs - You Angel You, Wedding Song, Forever Young - were simply adequate, and the rest was far less than that."
- Dave Marsh, Rolling Stone

"To me, Planet Waves sounds like nothing so much as a rough draft of an unfinished work, a sketch of planned painting, something to be worked on, not released."
– Jon Landau, Rolling Stone

Bob Dylan - Blood on the Tracks (1975)
"The long songs, particularly, suffer from flat, tangled imagery, and the music, with all its hints at the old glory, is often incompetently performed.
I suppose it's all a matter of what you're willing to settle for."
- Dave Marsh, Rolling Stone

"It's his best album since Blonde on Blonde, but not nearly as good.
To compare the new album to Blonde on Blonde at all is to imply that people will treasure it as deeply and for as long.
They won't."
– Jon Landau, Rolling Stone

Grateful Dead - American Beauty (1970)
"The band's attempts at pop, rock and country are rendered effortlessly irritating and stodgy by the band's lack of a crisp rhythm section and/or a single competent vocalist."
- Dave Marsh, Rolling Stone

Richard Hell & The Voidoids - Blank Generation (1977)
"In the first place, Jack Kerouac said everything here first, and far better. In the second place, Hell is about as whining as Verlaine is pretentious."
- Dave Marsh, Rolling Stone

Jimi Hendrix - Axis: Bold as Love (1967)
"Jimi Hendrix sounds like a junk heap. His songs too often are basically a bore, and the Experience also shares with Cream the problem of vocal ability."
- Jim Miller, Rolling Stone

Jimi Hendrix – Monterey Performance (1967)
"Hendrix is a psychedelic Uncle Tom. Grunting and groaning on the brink of sham orgasm, he made his way through five or six almost indistinguishable songs, occasionally flicking an anteater tongue at that great crotch in the sky. He also played what everybody seems to call 'heavy' guitar; in this case, that means he was loud. I suppose Hendrix's act can be seen as a consistently vulgar parody of rock theatrics, but I don't feel I have to like it. Anyhow, he can't sing."
– Robert Christgau

Buddy Holly (1936-1959)
"The biggest no-talent I ever worked with."
– Decca's Paul Cohen, after declining to renew Holly's contract.
Holly was later referred to as:
"The single most influential creative force in early rock and roll."

Journey - Escape (1981)
"A dead end for San Francisco area rock. The band made records perfectly calculated to be inserted into FM radio playlists: Stepford Wives rock, dead on its feet without any awareness of the utter triviality (not to mention banality) of such a scheme."
- Dave Marsh, Rolling Stone

When singer Steve Perry was asked about Marsh, he said:
"An unusual little man who all too often thinks that his subjective opinions translate to inarguable fact."

Led Zeppelin (1968-1980)
"I don't think the critics could understand what we were doing."
- Jimmy Page

Led Zeppelin - Led Zeppelin (1969) Debut record
*"[Plant is] as foppish as Rod Stewart, but he's nowhere near so exciting.
[Page is] a very limited producer and a writer of weak, unimaginative songs.
In their willingness to waste their considerable talent on unworthy material the Zeppelin has produced an album which is sadly reminiscent of [Jeff Beck's] Truth.
It would seem that, if they're to help fill the void created by the demise of Cream, they will have to find a producer (and editor) and some material worthy of their collective attention. Alternates between prissy Robert Plant's howled vocals fronting an acoustic guitar and driving choruses of the band running down a four-chord progression
while John Bonham smashes his cymbals on every beat."*
- John Mendelsohn, Rolling Stone

Led Zeppelin – Tour Review (1972)
*"Zeppelin's demeanor, like that of most of these groups, was loud, impersonal, exhibitionistic, violent, and often insane.
Watching them at a recent concert I saw little more than Plant's imitations of sexuality and Page's unwillingness to sustain a musical idea for more than a few measures. I got a sense that the real mood of the band is ennui.
I sat there thinking that rock could not go on like this."*
– Jon Landau

Led Zeppelin - Houses of the Holy (1973)
*"Houses of the Holy is one of the dullest and most confusing albums I've heard this year.
Over the Hills and Far Away is cut from the same mold as Stairway To Heaven, but without that song's torrid guitar solo it languishes in Dullsville —
just like the first five minutes of Stairway.
The whole premise of 'graduated heaviness' (upon which both songs were built) really goes to show just how puerile and rudimentary this group can get when forced to scrounge for its own material.
One would think that the group that stole Whole Lotta Love, et al., might acquire an idea or two along the way, but evidently they weren't looking.
When you really get down to it, Led Zeppelin hasn't come up with a consistent crop of heavy metal spuds since their second album. An occasional zinger like When the Levee Breaks isn't enough, especially when there are so many other groups today that don't bullshit around with inferior tripe like Stairway To Heaven."*
- Gordon Fletcher, Rolling Stone

Lynyrd Skynyrd – Second Helping (1974)
"This group is frequently compared to the Allman Brothers but it lacks that band's sophistication and professionalism. If a song doesn't feel right to the Brothers, they work on it until it does; if it isn't right to Lynyrd Skynyrd, they are more likely to crank up their amps and blast their way through the bottleneck."
– Gordon Fletcher, Rolling Stone

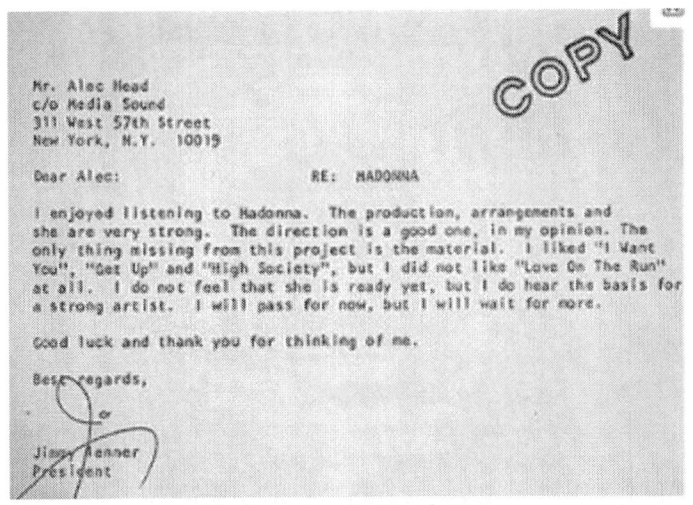

> Mr. Alec Head
> c/o Media Sound
> 311 West 57th Street
> New York, N.Y. 10019
>
> Dear Alec: RE: MADONNA
>
> I enjoyed listening to Madonna. The production, arrangements and she are very strong. The direction is a good one, in my opinion. The only thing missing from this project is the material. I liked "I Want You", "Get Up" and "High Society", but I did not like "Love On The Run" at all. I do not feel that she is ready yet, but I do hear the basis for a strong artist. I will pass for now, but I will wait for more.
>
> Good luck and thank you for thinking of me.
>
> Best regards,
>
> Jimmy Ienner
> President

Madonna's rejection letter.

Bob Marley & The Wailers – Exodus (1977)
"There is a contradiction here between the enormous abilities of the Wailers and the flatness of the material Bob Marley has given them to work with. The more I listen to this album, the more I am seduced by the playing of the band; at the same time, the connection I want to make with the music is subverted by overly familiar lyric themes unredeemed by wit or color, and by the absence of emotion in Marley's voice. There are some well-crafted lines here, but given Marley's singing, they don't come across. The precise intelligence one hears in every note of music cannot make up for its lack of drama, and that lack is Marley's."
- Greil Marcus, Rolling Stone

Bob Marley & The Wailers – Kaya (1978)
"This is quite possibly the blandest set of reggae music I have ever heard... dishing up potential Hall and Oates covers like Waiting in Vain is walking a mighty shaky tightrope."
– Lester Bangs, Rolling Stone

Van Morrison – Hard Nose The Highway (1973)
"A failed sidestep."
– Dave Marsh, Rolling Stone

Van Morrison - Veedon Fleece (1974)
"Veedon Fleece flounders in Morrison's own clichés. Throughout, Morrison suffers from wobbly pitch, several abortive experiments (the falsetto on Who Was That Masked Man) and a familiar tendency to mumble rather than enunciate. Too often he suggests a pinched vocal nerve drowning in porridge. This is pompous tripe."
- Jim Miller, Rolling Stone

Wolfgang Amadeus Mozart (1756-1791)
Mozart began composing at the age of five.
In his short life, he created more than 600 pieces of music.
Many were later acknowledged to be among the best ever created.
While alive, he enjoyed only minor notoriety and almost no financial success.
He died penniless at age 35.

Minutemen - What Makes a Man Start Fires? (1983)
*"The band's knotty, bass-driven rhythms are as static and unswinging
as its lyrics are strident and humorless."*
- J.D. Considine, Rolling Stone

Nirvana – Nevermind (1991)
"Most of Nevermind is packed with generic punk-pop that had been done by countless acts from Iggy Pop to the Red Hot Chili Peppers…the band has little or nothing to say, settling for moronic ramblings by singer-lyricist Cobain."
– Steve Morse, The Boston Globe

Pearl Jam – Ten (1991) Debut record
"It goes to show that just about anything can be harnessed and packaged."
– David Browne, Entertainment Weekly

"Trying to steal money from young alternative kids' pockets."
-NME

"San Francisco ballroom music. B-"
- Robert Christgau

Katy Perry
Perry's debut record sold an estimated 200 copies before her label folded.
She later signed with Island/Def Jam who shelved her record & then dropped her.
Perry signed with Columbia Records but was soon dropped by them as well.
She has now sold over 11 million records and 81 million singles worldwide.

Pink Floyd - Dark Side Of The Moon (1973)
"Snoozefest."
– Robert Christgau

Pink Floyd - Wish You Were Here (1975)
*"Their treatment is so solemn that you have to ask what the point is.
If your use of the machinery isn't alive enough to transcend its solemn hum
- even if that hum is your subject - then you're automatically trapped.
In offering not so much as a hint of liberation,
that's where this album leaves Pink Floyd."*
- Ben Edmonds, Rolling Stone

Pixies - Surfer Rosa (1988)
"These big-time fringe-rock avatars resemble a late-'70s heavy-metal outfit: okay, but nowhere near as dangerous - or as bad - as they're supposed to be."
- Mark Coleman, Rolling Stone

The Pogues - If I Should Fall From Grace With God (1988)
*"The group comes across as loutish buffoons, portraying Irish culture as little more than drunken dissolution. That the cover photo uses trick editing to slip James Joyce into their ranks should tell you something of the Pogues' ambition;
it's doubtful, though, that Joyce would have resorted to lyrics like
'You scumbag/You maggot/You cheap lousy faggot.'"*
- J.D. Considine, Rolling Stone

Iggy Pop - The Idiot (1977) Debut solo record
"By the time Iggy got this far, his maniacal inspiration was gone."
- Dave Marsh, Rolling Stone

Elvis Presley - (1935-1977)
"You ain't going nowhere, son. You ought to go back to driving a truck."
– Eddie Bond, rejecting Elvis' audition (April, 1954).

"They told me I couldn't sing."
– Elvis on why he failed an audition for local group *"The Songfellows"* (1954).

On the evening of July 5, 1954, 19-year-old Elvis Presley,
a $40 a week truck driver for Crown Electric,
walked into Sun Records for a recording session.
After a long night produced nothing particularly special,
guitarist Scotty Moore and bass player Bill Black were packing up to go home.
Elvis grabbed his guitar and *"started goofing off"* in his own unique way, singing:
"That's All Right".
The rest is history.

Queen - A Night at the Opera (1975)
"The group's flamboyance couldn't compensate for the weakness of its songwriting."
- Dave Marsh, Rolling Stone

Queen - A Day at the Races (1976)
"Blessed with Freddie Mercury's passable pop voice and guitarist Brian May, who manages to fragment and reassemble the guitar styles of Jimmy Page, Jeff Beck and Eric Clapton in interesting, if pedestrian, ways."
- Dave Marsh, Rolling Stone

Queen – Jazz (1978)
"Queen may be the first truly fascist rock band.
The whole thing makes me wonder why anyone would indulge these creeps
and their polluting ideas."
- Dave Marsh, Rolling Stone

Radiohead – OK Computer (1997)
"Radiohead wouldn't know a tragic hero if they were cramming for their A levels,
and their idea of soul is Bono, who they imitate further at the risk of looking even more
ridiculous than they already do. So instead they pickle Thom E. Yorke's vocals in enough
electronic marginal distinction to feed a coal town for a month.
Their art-rock has much better sound effects than the Floyd snoozefest Dark Side of the
Moon, but it's less sweeping and just as arid. I guarantee that it will not occupy the charts
for 10 years. In fact, only because the Brits seized EMI
does it have a chance to last through Christmas."
- Robert Christgau

Lou Reed - Transformer (1972)
"He should forget this artsy-fartsy kind of homo stuff."
- Nick Tosches, Rolling Stone

Lou Reed - Berlin (1973)
"Lou Reed's Berlin is a disaster, taking the listener into a distorted and degenerate
demimonde of paranoia, schizophrenia, degradation, pill-induced violence and suicide.
There are certain records that are so patently offensive that one wishes to take some kind of
physical vengeance on the artists that perpetrate them.
Reed's only excuse for this kind of performance (which isn't really performed as much as
spoken and shouted over Bob Ezrin's limp production) can only be that this was
his last shot at a once-promising career. Goodbye, Lou."
- Stephen Davis, Rolling Stone

"Barely a minor artist."
– Dave Marsh, Rolling Stone

The Rolling Stones - Sticky Fingers (1971)
"Middle-level Rolling Stones competence.
The low points aren't that low, but the high points, with one exception aren't that high.
I suppose somewhere along the line they thought of calling the album Dead Flowers
which would have justified this cut's presence at some level.
Despite its parodistic intentions, the mere thought of the Stones
doing straight country music is simply appalling.
And they do it so poorly, especially the lead guitar. On Sticky Fingers, it doesn't really sound
like they are doing what they want to. The two million hours they joke about spending on
this record must have surely resulted from uncertainty about what it was
they wanted to hear when they were through."
- Jon Landau, Rolling Stone

The Rolling Stones - Exile on Main St. (1972)
"Exile On Main Street spends its four sides shading the same song in as many variations as there are Rolling Stone ready-mades to fill them.
The fact that they take a minimum of chances, even given the room of their first double album set, tends to dull that finish a bit.
Exile On Main Street is the Rolling Stones at their most dense and impenetrable.
[It] appears to take up where Sticky Fingers left off, with the Stones attempting to deal with their problems and once again slightly missing the mark.
I still think the great Stones album of their mature period is yet to come.
Hopefully, Exile On Main Street will give them the solid footing they need to open up, and with a little horizon-expanding, they might even deliver it to us the next time around."
- Lenny Kaye, Rolling Stone

Bob Seger – Against The Wind (1980)
"Absolutely cowardly."
- Dave Marsh, Rolling Stone

Simon & Garfunkel - Bridge Over Troubled Water (1970)
"All the campus folkies were in a tizzy. The big day had finally arrived! After two years - two whole years - of waiting they finally had a new Simon & Garfunkel album to mull over. That the duo could only come up with 11 new songs in two years didn't seem to bother those fans. That nearly all of those songs were hopelessly mediocre fazed them even less."
- Gregg Mitchell, Rolling Stone

Sex Pistols Pretty Vacant/No Fun (1977)
"Pretty Vacant"/"No Fun", their newest single (a debut album is on the way), is a disappointment, coming off the angry excitement and comparative polish of God Save the Queen. Pretty Vacant' falls into the same pit that has swallowed so much promising Seventies music: bottom-heavy engineering that overboosts the bass tones at the expense of the guitars and vocals. What comes out is a clumsy, leaden blur."
- Charley Walters, Rolling Stone

Michelle Shocked - Short Sharp Shocked (1988)
"So full of musical posturing and ideological hectoring that it's hard to imagine anyone mistaking [it] for entertainment, much less art."
- J.D. Considine, Rolling Stone

The Smiths - The Smiths (1984) Debut record
"A lot of people who might otherwise have celebrated this British quartet's succinct rock & roll approach were utterly repelled by the brooding, obsessive persona of the band's bard-in-residence. The debut album lays everything on the table: endless potential and glaring pretensions, side by side."
- Mark Coleman, Rolling Stone

Bruce Springsteen – Greetings From Asbury Park (1973)
"Old Bruce makes a point of letting us know that he's from one of the scuzziest, most useless and plain uninteresting sections of Jersey.
He sort of catarrh-mumbles his ditties in a disgruntled mushmouth sorta like Robbie Robertson on Quaaludes with Dylan barfing down the back of his neck."
- Lester Bangs, Rolling Stone

Bruce Springsteen - Darkness on the Edge of Town (1978)
"Something in the Night and Streets of Fire are overwrought,
soggy, all but unlistenable.
An important minor artist or a rather flawed and inconsistent major one."
– Robert Christgau

Cat Stevens – Tea for the Tillerman (1970)
"My big problems with this record are no doubt why it's a hit: the artificially ripened singing, which goes down like a store-bought banana daiquiri,
and the insufferable sexist condescension of Wild World."
– Robert Christgau

Cat Stevens - Teaser and the Firecat (1971)
"Appears to be one of those composers who does not develop, who holds no surprises."
-Timothy Crouse, Rolling Stone

"Just one step away from monotony."
- Stephen Holden, Rolling Stone

"Hokey hippie mysticism."
– Mark Coleman, Rolling Stone

Igor Stravinsky (1882-1971) The Rite Of Spring (1913)
"A laborious and puerile barbarity."
– Le Figaro

"The work of a madman."
– Italian Composer Puccini

When Stravinsky debuted *The Rite of Spring*, audiences rioted.
It's now considered one of the most groundbreaking musical works ever.
TIME Magazine later named Stravinsky as one of
The 100 most influential people of the 20th century.

U2 – October (1981)
"What a stupid band to expect purity from."
- Robert Christgau

U2 - The Unforgettable Fire (1984)
*"U2 flickers and nearly fades, its fire banked by a misconceived production strategy and occasional interludes of soggy, songless self-indulgence. This is not a 'bad' album, but neither is it the irrefutable beauty the band's fans anticipated.
What happened?"*
- Kurt Loder, Rolling Stone

U2 – The Joshua Tree (1987)
*"Bono's work is marred throughout by sobbing affectation that approaches the clichéd bleating rhetoric all too familiar from American 'corporate-rock' bands.
If Bono's vocals represent a miscalculation, so, one imagines, does the pervasively depressed tone of this album as a whole. Once upon a time, rock-and-roll was cheerful music, meant to galvanize teen-agers into dancing or worse. The Joshua Tree puts U2 squarely into the camp of what Jon Pareles last week called 'mope rock.'"*
- John Rockwell, The New York Times

Van Halen – Van Halen (1978) Debut record
"For some reason Warner's wants us to know that this is the biggest bar band in the San Fernando Valley ... The term becomes honorific when the music belongs in a bar. This music belongs on an aircraft carrier."
– Robert Christgau

*"In three years, Van Halen is going to be fat and self-indulgent and disgusting ... follow[ing] Deep Purple and Led Zeppelin right into the toilet.
In the meantime, they are likely to be a big deal."*
– Charles M. Young, Rolling Stone

Van Halen - Van Halen II (1979)
*"A Southern California band that grinds out a variety of variations on the basic 'Louie Louie' thump theme, most notably a version of the Kinks' earlier variation,
You Really Got Me. The second album is as imaginative as its title."*
- Dave Marsh, Rolling Stone

Violent Femmes - Violent Femmes (1983) Debut record
"Gano works up a convincing (if not compelling) neurotic fury on three-chord throbbers like Add It Up. Like most Lou Reed disciples, however, he tends to sound unpleasantly nasal on the inevitable, talky mid-tempo melodramas."
- Mark Coleman, Rolling Stone

Neil Young - Comes a Time (1978)
"Young remains a minor artist."
- Dave Marsh, Rolling Stone

Bono/U2 Rejection letter.

RSO Records (U.K.) Limited
A Division of the Robert Stigwood Group Ltd.

67 Brook Street London W1Y 1YE England
Telephone 01-629 9121
Cables Stigwood London W1
Telex 264267

Mr. P. Hewson,
10 Cobewood Road,
Dublin 11

10th May 1979,

Dear Mr. Hewson,

Thank you for submitting your tape of 'U2' to RSO, we have listened with careful consideration, but feel it is not suitable for us at present.

We wish you luck with your future career.

Yours sincerely,

*ALEXANDER SINCLAIR

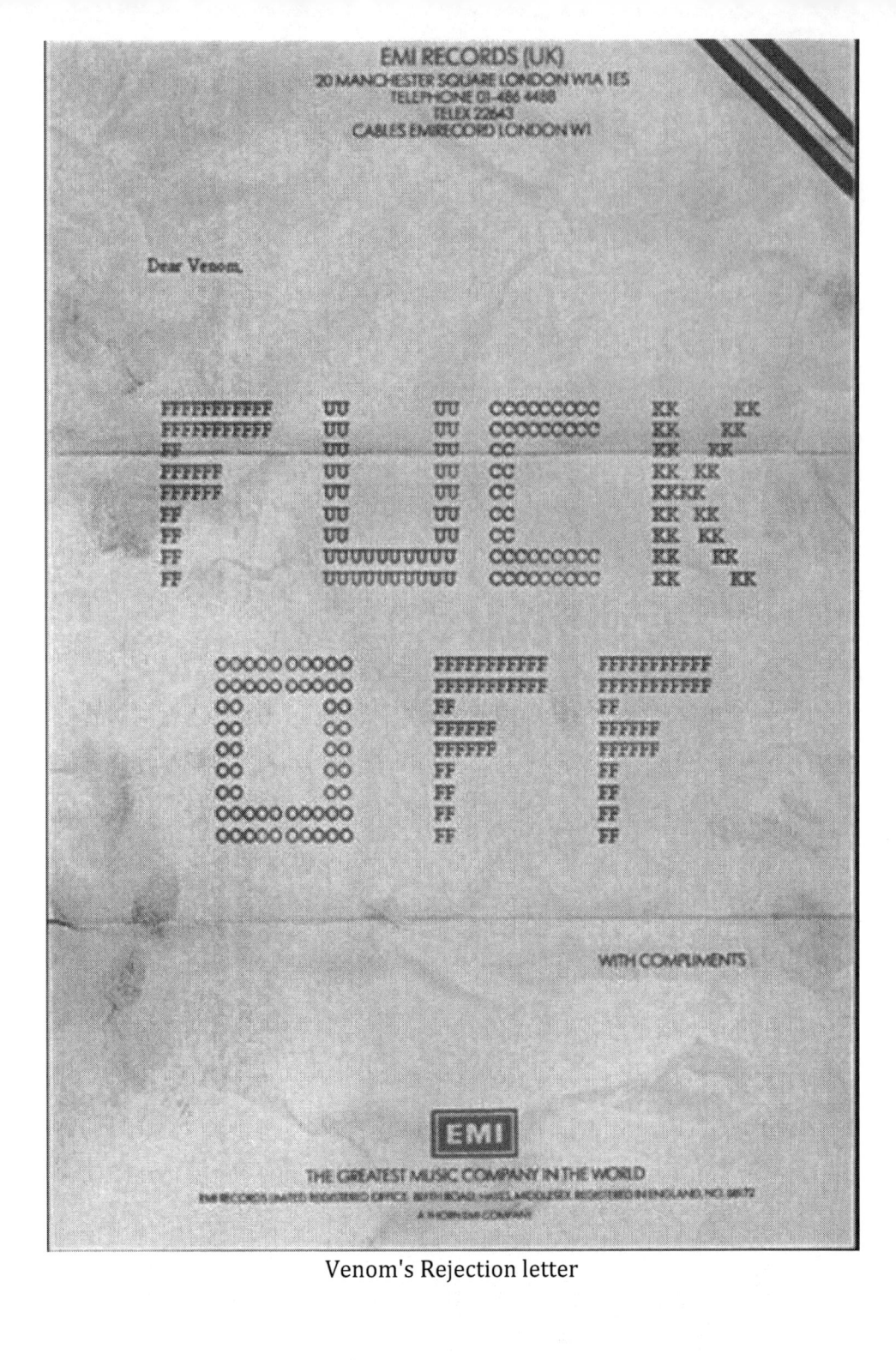

EMI RECORDS (UK)
20 MANCHESTER SQUARE LONDON W1A 1ES
TELEPHONE 01-486 4488
TELEX 22643
CABLES EMIRECORD LONDON W1

Dear Venom,

```
FFFFFFFFFFF    UU      UU    CCCCCCCCC    KK      KK
FFFFFFFFFFF    UU      UU    CCCCCCCCC    KK    KK
FF             UU      UU    CC           KK  KK
FFFFFF         UU      UU    CC           KK KK
FFFFFF         UU      UU    CC           KKKK
FF             UU      UU    CC           KK KK
FF             UU      UU    CC           KK  KK
FF             UUUUUUUUUU    CCCCCCCCC    KK    KK
FF             UUUUUUUUUU    CCCCCCCCC    KK      KK
```

```
OOOOO OOOOO      FFFFFFFFFFF    FFFFFFFFFFF
OOOOO OOOOO      FFFFFFFFFFF    FFFFFFFFFFF
OO       OO      FF             FF
OO       OO      FFFFFF         FFFFFF
OO       OO      FFFFFF         FFFFFF
OO       OO      FF             FF
OO       OO      FF             FF
OOOOO OOOOO      FF             FF
OOOOO OOOOO      FF             FF
```

WITH COMPLIMENTS

EMI

THE GREATEST MUSIC COMPANY IN THE WORLD
EMI RECORDS LIMITED REGISTERED OFFICE. BLYTH ROAD, HAYES, MIDDLESEX. REGISTERED IN ENGLAND, NO. 68172
A THORN EMI COMPANY

Venom's Rejection letter

PRO TIPS

"Make mistakes, make mistakes, make mistakes.
Just make sure they're _your_ mistakes."
- Fiona Apple

"To some extent I happily don't know what I'm doing.
I feel that it's an artist's responsibility to trust that."
- David Byrne

"You build on failure. You use it as a steppingstone. Close the door on the past.
You don't try to forget the mistakes, but you don't dwell on it.
You don't let it have any of your energy, or any of your time, or any of your space."
- Johnny Cash

"If you pour some music on whatever's wrong, it'll sure help out."
- Levon Helm

"The fact that we're standing here tonight, the fact that we're able to hold this,
it just proves no matter how far out your dreams are, it's possible.
And fair play to those who dare to dream and don't give up."
- Markéta Irglová's Academy Award® acceptance speech for _Once_.

"God sent me on earth. He send me to do something, and nobody can stop me.
If God want to stop me, then I stop. Man never can."
- Bob Marley

"A lot of people make money off of fear and negativity and any way they can feed it to you is
to their benefit in a lot of ways. You can't avoid it completely;
You have to be open enough that shit doesn't stick on you, it goes through,
because you are gonna be hit and bombarded all the time with negativity.
You just let things go on through without trying to stop them or block them."
- Willie Nelson

"It's like if you plant something in the concrete and if it grows and the rose petals got all
kinds of scratches and marks, you 'ain't gonna say, 'Damn, look at all the scratches and
marks on the rose.' You're gonna be like, 'Damn, a rose grew from the concrete?'"
- Tupac Shakur

"The best revenge is massive success."
– Frank Sinatra

"There's always that argument to make – that you're in better company historically
if people don't understand what you're doing."
- Elliott Smith

PERFORMERS

*"If only I'd known my differentness would be an asset,
then my earlier life would have been much easier."*
- Bette Midler

Dame Julie Andrews, DBE
"She's not photogenic enough for film."
–MGM screen test rejection (1947).
Andrews later starred in *Mary Poppins* and *The Sound of Music*.
She won an Oscar® for Best Actress in 1965.

Fred Astaire (1899–1987)
"Can't act. Slightly bald. Also dances."
- Burt Grady, RKO talent dept. after Astaire's first screen test.
Astaire later received an AFI Life Achievement Award,
an Academy Award®, a Grammy Lifetime Achievement Award
and Kennedy Center Honors.
"The history of dance on film begins with Astaire."
– Gene Kelly
"Simply the greatest, most imaginative dancer of our time."
–Rudolf Nureyev
"What do dancers think of Fred Astaire? It's no secret. We hate him. He gives us a complex because he's too perfect. His perfection is an absurdity. It's too hard to face."
- Mikhail Baryshnikov

Lucille Ball (1911-1989)
*"Lucy's wasting her time and ours.
She's too shy and reticent to put her best foot forward."*
– Letter to her mother from Lucy's performing arts high-school.
"Try any other profession. Any other."
- John Murray Anderson drama teacher to Lucille Ball (1927).
Lucy was nominated for 13 Emmy's
She received a Lifetime Achievement Award from The Kennedy Center in 1986.

Michael Caine
"You will be a laborer all your life."
- His school Headmaster.
Caine has won 2 Academy Awards®, is a Commander of The British Empire
and was Knighted by the Queen.

Charlie Chaplin (1889-1977)
"The most dramatic of all the rags to riches stories ever told."
- Chaplin's biographer
Chaplin's childhood was fraught with poverty and hardship.
He was sent to a workhouse when he was 7-years-old,
then housed at the Central London School for paupers, which he later recalled as:
"A forlorn existence."
He was briefly reunited with his mother in 1898, before she was forced to readmit Charlie
and his brother to an institution for destitute children.
In September 1898, Chaplin's mother was committed to a mental asylum.

For the two months she was there, Chaplin and his brother Sydney were sent to live with their father, an alcoholic whom the young boys hardly knew.
Charles Sr. died two years later, at 38 years old, from cirrhosis of the liver.
His mother was discharged from the asylum but in 1903 became ill again.
Chaplin, then 14, had to return her to the asylum.
He was homeless until his brother Sydney returned from the Navy.
Chaplin began performing and eventually adopted "the Tramp" character.
He made suggestions for films he appeared in but his ideas were typically dismissed.
While filming *Mabel at the Wheel*, he clashed with the director and was nearly fired.
Chaplin was allowed to direct a film, only after he promised to pay $1,500 if it failed.
It was a success.
He went on to write/direct/produce/edit/star in & compose the music for his films.
He is now considered one of the most important figures in the history of cinema.

Harrison Ford
His first role was a bit part as a bellboy in a 1966 movie. The producer told Ford:
"You're never gonna make it in this business, kid.
The first time Tony Curtis was in a movie, he delivered a bag of groceries.
You took one look at the guy and said 'that's a movie star!'"
Ford replied: *"I thought you were supposed to think 'that's a grocery delivery boy?!'"*
Unhappy with the roles being offered to him, Ford became a self-taught carpenter.
After George Lucas hired him to build cabinets for his home, he gave Ford a small part in *American Graffiti*. In 1975, Lucas hired him to read lines with actors auditioning for *Star Wars*. Spielberg was there, and noticed Ford might be a good fit for Han Solo.

Phil Hartman (1948-1998)
In 1986 he was rejected for a job as the announcer on The New Hollywood Squares. As a result, he was available to audition for Saturday Night Live soon after.
He later said: *"I sometimes wonder where I'd be if I had gotten that announcing job."*

Harvey Keitel
He was rejected 8 years in a row before he was accepted into the Actors Studio. Now, he's the Co-President.
He was also fired as the lead in *Apocalypse Now* after filming had commenced.

Marilyn Monroe (1926-1962)
"Fear is stupid. So are regrets."
Born to a single, mentally unstable mother, Norma Jean Mortensen was declared a ward of the state and raised in foster homes.
While trying to start her career, modeling agents told her she should consider becoming a secretary instead.

Jeanne Moreau
Moreau was told by a casting director that she wasn't pretty enough to be in films.
In 1958, the press called her *"The new Bardot."*
She has starred in nearly 100 films and received numerous awards.

Sidney Poitier
*"Why don't you stop wasting people's time
and go out and become a dishwasher or something?"*
- Casting director
In 1964, Poitier became the first person of color to win an
Academy Award® for Best Actor.

Jerry Seinfeld
After quitting as a light bulb telemarketer, Seinfeld booked his first stand-up gig.
When he first came out to perform, he froze and was booed off the stage.
Later in his career, he learned he had been fired from a role on the sitcom *Benson* when he showed up for work and discovered his part was absent from the script.
He's now worth an estimated $800 million.

Sylvester Stallone
Stallone was a homeless, struggling actor with 1,500 rejections, sleeping in the Port Authority Bus Terminal when he performed in a soft-core porn film for $200.
"It was either do that movie or rob someone because, I was at the very end of my rope."
He turned to screenwriting out of frustration at being unable to land acting jobs.
In 1975, poverty forced him to sell his beloved dog Butkus at a liquor store for $50.
He later said it was the lowest point in his life.
After watching the Ali/Wepner fight in March, 1975, Stallone wrote *Rocky* in 3 days.
The script was rejected numerous times before producers Robert Chartoff and Irwin Winkler offered to buy it for $100,000 on the condition that "a star" play the lead.
Although he had only $106 in the bank at the time, Stallone refused. Later saying:

"I never would have sold it. I told my wife that I'd rather bury it in the back yard and let the caterpillars play Rocky. I would have hated myself for selling out, the way we hate most people for selling out. My wife agreed, and said she'd be willing to move to a trailer in the middle of a swamp if need be."

The producers eventually raised their offer to $265,000 and 5% of the profits
if Stallone would step aside. He again refused.
The producers finally let him play the lead for $35,000 and 10% of the profits.
Stallone returned to the liquor store and bought Butkus back for $3,000.
That's <u>really him</u>, playing himself, in the movie.
The film earned $225 million and won three Oscars®, including Best Picture.

*"You know, if nothing else comes out of that film in the way of awards and accolades,
it will still show that an unknown quantity, a totally unmarketable person,
can produce a diamond in the rough, a gem.
And there are a lot more people like me out there, too."*
– Sylvester Stallone (1976).

PRO TIPS

*"Most of these critics are usually frustrated artists
and they criticize other people's art because they can't do it themselves.
It's a really disgusting job. They must feel horrible inside."*
- Rosanna Arquette

*"I don't think the goal is, 'How big a star did you ever become?'
I think the goal is, 'Were you able to express yourself?'"*
- Albert Brooks

"When you write from your gut and let the stuff stay flawed and don't let anybody tell you to make it better, it can end up looking like nothing else."
- Louis C.K.

"Nothing will stop you being creative so effectively as the fear of making a mistake."
- John Cleese

"Pure entertainment is not an egotistical lady singing boring songs onstage for two hours and people in tuxes clapping whether they like it or not. It's the real performers on the street who can hold people's attention and keep them from walking away."
- Andy Kaufman

*"The most exciting acting tends to happen in roles
you never thought you could play."*
- John Lithgow

*"You want to be a bit compulsive in your art or craft or whatever you do.
You want to be focused on it."*
- Steve Martin

"Well behaved women rarely make history."
- Marilyn Monroe

"Life shrinks or expands in proportion to one's courage."
- Jack Nicholson

"Fear is the base of what everybody does wrong in their lives."
- Elaine Stritch

"If you're creating anything at all, it's really dangerous to care what people think."
Kristen Wiig

"You're only given a little spark of madness. You mustn't lose it."
- Robin Williams

SPORTS

*"My motto was always to keep swinging.
Whether I was in a slump or feeling badly
or having trouble off the field...
the only thing to do was keep swinging."*
- **Hank Aaron**

Glenn Cunningham (1909-1988)
At the age of 8, Cunningham's legs were badly burned in a schoolhouse fire.
His brother was killed in the fire.
Doctors recommended amputation of both of his legs.
His parents wouldn't allow it.
Doctors told him that he would never walk normally.
He ran for the United States at the 1932 Olympic games.
In 1934, he set the world record for the fastest mile.
He ran again in the 1936 Olympics and set the world record for the 800 meter.

Jack Johnson (1878-1946)
"If the black man wins, thousands and thousands of his ignorant brothers will misinterpret
his victory as justifying claims to much more than mere
physical equality with their white neighbors."
– The New York Times (1910)
During an era of tremendous racism, Johnson became the first
African American world heavyweight boxing champion.
At his funeral, his wife said:
"He faced the world unafraid. There wasn't anybody or anything he feared."

Michael Jordan
*"I have missed more than 9,000 shots in my career. I have lost almost 300 games.
On 26 occasions I have been entrusted to take the game winning shot, and I missed.
I have failed over and over and over again in my life. And that is why I succeed."*
When he first tried out for his high school basketball team, Jordan was rejected.
He has since been called the greatest basketball player ever.

Jeremy Lin
Lin received no college scholarship offers and was undrafted after college.
He began his career with the Golden State Warriors, rarely played and was demoted to
the "D" (development) league, three times before being cut.
He was then picked up by the Houston Rockets, but waived in pre-season.
The Knicks picked Lin up, but put him in the D-league before recalling him in 2012.
He asked the team's chaplain before his first game: *"Can you pray I don't get cut?"*
Lin scored 136 points in his first five games, the most ever scored by an NBA player.

Manny Pacquiao
Born into extreme poverty in the Philippines, he left home at age14 because
his father cooked and ate Manny's pet dog.
He lived on the streets of Manila and slept in a cardboard box.
At 16, 4'11" and 98 lbs., with weights in his pockets to make the limit, he turned pro.
Pacquiao eventually became the world champion in eight different boxing divisions.
He's now one of the wealthiest Filipino's and donates substantially to the needy.

Wilma Rudolph (1940-1994)
Born prematurely, Wilma was a victim of polio as a child.
She wore a leg brace until the age of 9 and orthopedic shoes until age 11.
She later battled scarlet fever.
Rudolph's only dream was to be able to run like normal children.
She eventually became the fastest woman in the world.
In 1960, she was the first woman to win 3 gold medals in a single Olympics.

Babe Ruth (1895-1948)
"Never let the fear of striking out keep you from coming to bat."
For 30 years, he held the record for the most strikeouts.
For 52 years, he held the record for the most home runs.
"Every strike brings me closer to the next home run."
"I swing big, with everything I've got. I hit big or I miss big. I like to live as big as I can."
"If I'd tried for them dinky singles I could've batted around six hundred."
He's considered to be one of the greatest baseball players in history.

Jim Thorpe (1888-1953)
"You, sir, are the greatest athlete in the world"
– King Gustav V of Sweden.
"Thanks, King."
- Jim Thorpe, receiving his Olympic gold medals.
Part Native American, Thorpe contended with racism all his life.
He won 2 gold medals at the 1912 Olympic games.
They were revoked for 30 years, before being restored after his death.
He was a professional football, baseball and basketball player.
He died a broke alcoholic in 1953.
In 2000, Thorpe was voted Greatest Athlete of the 20th Century.

Johnny Unitas (1933-2002)
"You'll get murdered out there."
- Notre Dame coach, rejecting Unitas because he was too skinny.
As a 9th round pick for the Steelers in 1955, he was released in pre-season.
The coach felt he wasn't smart enough to play.
He worked construction and played semi-pro for $6 a game to support his family.
In 1956, Unitas accompanied a friend to Baltimore for a tryout with the Colts.
He tried out too.
His Uncle told him not to, fearing if the Colts passed, his pro chances would be over.
They signed him.
In 1959 he became the NFL's first MVP.
He is now considered to be one of the best NFL players ever.

PRO TIPS

"Impossible is just a big word thrown around by small men who find it easier to live in the world they've been given than to explore the power they have to change it. Impossible is not a fact. It's an opinion. Impossible is not a declaration. It's a dare. Impossible is potential. Impossible is temporary. Impossible is nothing."
– Muhammad Ali

"You are never really playing an opponent. You are playing yourself, your own highest standards, and when you reach your limits, that is real joy."
- Arthur Ashe

"I was told over and over again that I would never be successful, that I was not going to be competitive and the technique was simply not going to work.
All I could do was shrug and say 'We'll just have to see.'"
- Dick Fosbury, creator of the "back first" high-jump. He won an Olympic gold with it.

"You miss 100% of the shots you don't take."
– Wayne Gretzky

"Make sure your worst enemy doesn't live between your own two ears."
- Laird Hamilton

"You find that you have peace of mind and can enjoy yourself, get more sleep, and rest when you know that it was a 100% effort that you gave – win or lose."
- Gordie Howe

"It's not whether you get knocked down; it's whether you get back up."
– Vince Lombardi

"It isn't hard to be good from time to time in sports.
What is tough, is being good every day."
- Willie Mays

"I've always made a total effort, even when the odds seemed entirely against me.
I never quit trying; I never felt that I didn't have a chance to win."
– Arnold Palmer

"A trophy carries dust. Memories last forever."
- Mary Lou Retton

"It's hard to beat a person who never gives up."
- Babe Ruth

TELEVISION

*"It's the menace that everyone loves to hate
but can't seem to live without."*
- Paddy Chayevsky

Arrested Development - Season 1 (2003)
*"A marvelous cast, offbeat situations and innovative direction.
Your humble critic, however, finds one problem: It's not very funny."*
- The Philadelphia Inquirer

*"Despite some amusing bits involving the parents, there's a major problem:
Arrested Development isn't especially funny.
That's the one asset every successful sitcom must have."*
- Orlando Sentinel

Beavis and Butt-Head - Season 1 (1993)
*"There's a fine line between clever and stupid, as somebody says in This Is Spinal Tap, Rob
Reiner's cleverly stupid 'rockumentary.'
Beavis and Butt-head don't just walk that line: they live there."*
- The New York Times

Boardwalk Empire - Season 1 (2010)
*"Boardwalk Empire is at great pains to give viewers a sense that they are there,
and yet rarely did I feel engrossed in the show.
Even if its point is to show you the ugly side of fun,
Boardwalk Empire should be much more fun to watch."*
– The New Yorker

Breaking Bad - Season 1 (2008)
*"You can feel creator Vince Gilligan (of The X-Files) straining to build
an emblematic American fable and forgetting to fill in his story
with particularities and believable motivations."*
- The Boston Globe

*"Breaking could be a good study of acting, since Cranston and Aaron Paul
(as his partner, Jesse) get under the grimy skin of their characters.
But there's not enough of the good stuff,
like writing, directing, mood, cinematography - you get the point."*
- Chicago Sun-Times

Curb Your Enthusiasm - Season 1 (2000)
*"The humor is minutely observed, but the improv reminds you how much non-actor Jerry
Seinfeld benefited from comic backup and tight scripts."*
- TIME Magazine

"The project as a whole reeks of self-indulgence and vanity."
- San Diego Union-Tribune

Friends - Season 1 (1994)
"The trouble with Friends is that Cox is not strong enough as a comedian."
- Newsday

"Friends comes across like a 30-minute commercial for Dockers or Ikea or light beer, except it's smuttier. Another ghastly creation from professional panderers Marta Kauffman and David Crane, the witless duo who do Dream On for HBO,
Friends is more a scripted talk show than a sitcom.
You keep waiting for Sally Jessy or some other cluck to interrupt the jabbering.
The show is so bad that Sally Jessy would actually come as a relief."
- Tom Shales, Washington Post

Game Of Thrones - Season 1 (2011)
"Game of Thrones serves up a lot of confusion in the name of no larger or really relevant idea beyond sketchily fleshed-out notions that war is ugly,
families are insidious and power is hot.
If you are not averse to the Dungeons & Dragons aesthetic, the series might be worth the effort. If you are nearly anyone else, you will hunger for HBO to get back to the business of languages for which we already have a dictionary."
- Ginia Bellafante, The New York Times

"In a world that looks superficially medieval, various warriors and women with British accents fight to survive in a power struggle that has lasted thousands of years.
Thrones also has wolf pups, which is always cool.
But then we're back to the familiar favorites of the infantile."
- The Wall Street Journal

Louie - Season 1 (2010)
"Louie is so low-key that it has no discernible pulse.
To say it's unfunny is accurate (profoundly so) but also beside the point:
It's un-anything."
- Miami Herald

"We see his standup act and we laugh.
We watch this whole package and the laughs are sporadic.
Someday he may find the scripted sitcom that captures his humor. Not this time."
- The New York Daily News

Mad Men - Season 1 (2007)
"To steal from the old beer slogan,
(this show) looks great, (but it's) less filling (than it intends)."
- Newsday

"This series feel like a fifties leftover, chock-full of unimportant secrets."
- New York Magazine

"The costumes and sets are just ducky and highly evocative, but the people in and around them spoil the show, gum up the works and shatter veracity."
- Tom Shales, The Washington Post

"The mood is serious, not campy, and there aren't laugh-out-loud moments,
just a lot of groaners - at which point, the show simply becomes a reflection of its
characters: depressing."
- The New Republic

Seinfeld - Season 1 (1989)
"Lacking much in the way of attitude, the show seems obsolete and irrelevant.
What it boils down to is that Seinfeld, likable as he may be, is a mayonnaise clown in a world
that requires a little horseradish."
- USA Today

The Simpsons - Season 1 (1990)
"The Simpsons is strangely off-putting much of the time.
The drawings are grotesque without redeeming style or charm (characters have big beady
eyes, beaklike noses and spiky hair),
and the animation is crude even by TV's low-grade standards."
– Richard Zoglin, TIME Magazine

The Soprano's - Season 1 (1999)
"The Sopranos would have benefited from the editing required by network time
and content restraints, which would have made the rambling episodes tighter
and cleared them of their worst blood and exposed-breast excesses."
- USA Today

"A gangster's midlife crisis is a weak, unpalatable premise for a series.
The Sopranos makes an offer you can refuse."
- Orlando Sentinel

South Park - Season 1 (1997)
"It's dismissible juvenilia. A collection of poorly paced, lowest-common-denominator setups
that are not even sophomorically funny or scatologically goofy."
- The Hollywood Reporter

"To say that the series is not for everyone is lavish understatement.
The real question: Is it for anyone?"
- Tom Shales, The Washington Post

"It might help if the South Park kids had personalities,
but they're as one-dimensional as the show's cut-and-paste animation."
- Entertainment Weekly

The Wire – Season 1 (2002)
"The Wire looks and feels like an ordinary show from some other network that snuck on to
the air while the HBO execs' backs were turned."
– The New York Post

"After watching five hours of preview tapes, I'm interested to see how The Wire turns out. But without characters to care for, much less root for, I'm not exactly burning with curiosity -- the way I am with most of HBO's other series.
When it comes down to The Wire, this show falls short."
– The New York Daily News

The X-Files - Season 1 (1993)
"It's not quite sci-fi, not quite fantasy, and yet not quite realistic either.
It's not quite a show, is what it's not quite...You may get an urge to take a hike too, but pity the poor critic who has to sit there with a big grin on his face
and watch the whole stupid thing."
- Tom Shales, The Washington Post

PRO TIPS

"I think storytelling is all about children. We human beings love to hear stories being told - and it first happens when you're a kid."
- David Chase

"The first question: Is this two hours worth of story or a hundred hours worth of story? And in all honesty, I've written movies that have been made and the process has not been as satisfying as writing for television."
- Vince Gilligan

"Television is a very writer-driven business, and it's one of the few parts of entertainment where writers are treated with respect, only because they need you. If they didn't have to treat you with respect, they would be happy to dismiss you."
- Mitchell Hurwitz

"Here's the thing about movies, all movies end up on television. That's their life. Whether you like it or not, I don't care how much money you spend on it, or how big or broad the film is, or who the actors are in it, eventually it's all coming out of the box."
- Greg Kinnear

"The news media's silence, particularly television news, is reprehensible. If we knew as much about Darfur as we do about Michael Jackson, we might be able to stop these things from continuing."
- Nicholas D. Kristof

"Television provides the opportunity for an ongoing story - the opportunity to meld the cast and the characters and a world, and to spend more time there."
- David Lynch

"Because of how much movies cost, it's dangerous to be experimental on one film after the other. But we can experiment with television. We can do things that are fringe and bring ideas to the table that are offbeat and original."
- Steven Spielberg

"I've never been shocked by anything on television, except the news."
- Justin Theroux

"There's something to be said for going right into people's living rooms. I think actors have always loved that medium - you're right in there with people in their homes. A lot of very audacious work is being done on television."
- Sigourney Weaver

BAD CALLS

*"For God's sake, go down to reception and get rid of a lunatic who's down there.
He says he's got a machine for seeing by wireless!
Watch him — he may have a razor on him."*
- A Daily Express editor, when John Logie Baird showed up
to promote his new invention, the television (1925).

"So I repeat that while theoretically and technically television may be feasible, commercially and financially, I consider it an impossibility; a development of which we need not waste little time in dreaming."
- Lee DeForest, inventor (1926).

*"Television? The word is half Latin and half Greek.
No good can come of it."*
- British publisher/politician, Charles Prestwich Scott (c. 1928).

"Television won't be able to hold on to any market it captures after the first 6 months. People will soon get tired of staring at a plywood box every night."
- Darryl F. Zanuck, 20th Century Fox Executive (1946)

"Comedy on network television is dead. Forever. Bury it."
- ABC Entertainment president Lewis Erlicht rejecting The Cosby Show (1984).

"No segment of the audience was eager to watch the show again."
Test audience reaction to the *Seinfeld* pilot (1989).

"Pass."
ABC executives, rejecting *CSI* franchise creator Anthony Zuicker's pitch (1999).
Zuicker later named his production company: "Dare to Pass".

"Forget it, that's the worst idea I've ever heard, it will never work and it's too hard."
- Producer Robert Cochran's initial reaction to the concept for *24* (2001).

*"It's a period piece, it's never going to go anywhere.
We need you to make money and this isn't going to make money."*
-Christina Hendricks' talent agency, dropping her for taking *Mad Men* role (2007).

"OK...well....thank you for coming in."
- HBO executive, dismissing creator Vince Gilligan's pitch for *Breaking Bad (2007).*

WRITERS

*"There's nothing to stop a man from writing
unless that man stops himself.
If a man truly desires to write, then he will.
Rejection and ridicule will only strengthen him.
And the longer he is held back the stronger he will become,
like a mass of rising water against a dam.
There is no losing in writing, it will make your toes laugh as you sleep,
it will make you stride like a tiger, it will fire the eye
and put you face to face with death.
You will die a fighter, you will be honored in hell.
The luck of the word. Go with it, send it."*
- Charles Bukowski

Chinua Achebe - *Things Fall Apart (1958)*
"Fiction from African writers has no market potential."
- Publisher's rejection

In 1957, after writing his first novel by hand while living in Nigeria,
Achebe took advantage of a printed ad and sent it off to London to be typed.
After waiting months, he began to worry, as it was the only copy of his book.
He asked a friend who was to be visiting London to check on the progress.
When she arrived at the typists, she angrily confronted them after she found Achebe's
manuscript sitting in a pile, ignored. They quickly typed it up.
Achebe later noted that had his friend not intervened or if the book had been lost:
"I would have been so discouraged that I would probably have given up altogether."
After it was printed, the book was rejected many times.
Published in 1958 it became the most widely read book in African literature.
It has been translated into more than 50 languages
and is part of school curriculums around the world.

Richard Adams - *Watership Down (1972)*
"Older children will not like it because its language is too difficult."
- Rejection letter

After many rejections, one-man London publisher Rex Collings agreed to print it,
writing to an associate:
*"I've just taken on a novel about rabbits, one of them with extra-sensory perception.
Do you think I'm mad?"*
The associate responded that it was *"a mad risk"* and later wrote of Collings:
*"A bizarre book by an unknown writer, which had been turned down
by the major London publishers; but it was also dazzlingly brave and intuitive."*
Critical reception was mixed:
*"Banal Bunnies - It has about the same intellectual firepower as Dumbo.
Watership Down is an adventure story, no more than that: rather a swashbuckling crude
one to boot. There are virtuous rabbits and bad rabbits:
if that's allegory, Bonanza is an allegory."*
– The National Review.
Watership Down became one of the fastest-selling books in history and in a survey of the
British public, was voted one of the greatest books of all time.

Louisa May Alcott - *Little Women (1871)*
"Tell Louisa to stick to her teaching; she can never succeed as a writer."
- James T. Fields, editor of *The Atlantic Magazine*
Little Women was an immediate success, has never gone out of print and is one of the
most beloved children's books ever.

Sherwood Anderson – *Winesburg, Ohio (1919)*
"Far too gloomy for us."
– Rejection from publisher John Lane
It has become known as one of the best English-language novels of the 20th century.

Richard Bach - *Jonathan Livingston Seagull (1970)*
"Nobody will want to read a book about a seagull."
- One of twenty rejections
Macmillan agreed to publish it and Bach received a $2,000 advance.
It broke all sales records since *Gone with the Wind* and sold 45 million copies.
*"A book so banal that it had to be sold to adults; kids would have seen through it.
The Little Engine That Could is, by comparison, a work of some depth and ambition."*
– Roger Ebert, re; the film adaptation.

L. Frank Baum - *The Wonderful Wizard Of Oz (1900)*
"Too radical of a departure from traditional juvenile literature."
- Publisher's rejection
The book has sold millions of copies, been translated into over 50 languages and adapted into the classic 1939 film.

Fun Facts: - The name *OZ* came from Baum's file cabinet O-Z.
In 1957, Detroit's Library Director had it banned:
for having *"no value"* and reducing children's minds *"to a cowardly level."*
In 1986, Tennessee Christians filed a lawsuit opposing its teaching in public schools.
One parent said: *"I don't want my children seduced into godless supernaturalism."*

J.G. Ballard - *Crash (1973)*
"This author is beyond psychiatric help. Do not publish!"
– Rejection
Ballard takes this rejection as an indication of *"complete artistic success."*
The book is published, later becoming an award winning film.
In 1984 he writes *Empire of the Sun*.

James Baldwin - *Giovanni's Room (1956)*
"Hopelessly bad."
– Rejection from Knopf Publishers

Judy Blume
"Does not win in competition with others."
- Rejection from Highlights magazine

*"For 2 years I received nothing but rejections.
I still can't look at a copy of Highlights without wincing.
I would go to sleep at night feeling that I'd never be published.
But I'd wake up in the morning convinced I would be.
Each time I sent a story or book off to a publisher,
I would sit down and begin something new.
I was learning more with each effort. I was determined.
Determination and hard work are as important as talent."*
Her books have since sold more than 80 million copies
and been translated into 31 languages.

Jorge Luis Borges - (1899-1986)
"Utterly untranslatable."
– A Knopf rejection
In 1961, he won the Prix International Award. In 1968, he lectured at Harvard. His books have been translated into several languages, including English.

Emily Brontë, *Wuthering Heights* (1847)
"We know nothing in the whole range of our fictitious literature which presents such shocking pictures of the worst forms of humanity. There is not a single character which is not utterly hateful or thoroughly contemptible."
– Atlas (1848)

"How a human being could have attempted such a book as the present without committing suicide before he had finished a dozen chapters, is a mystery. It is a compound of vulgar depravity and unnatural horrors."
–Graham's Lady Magazine

Her first and only novel is now considered a masterpiece.

Dan Brown - *The Da Vinci Code (2003)*
"It is so badly written." – Rejection
Doubleday agrees to publish it and the novel has sold more than 80 million copies.

Pearl S. Buck - *The Good Earth (1931)*
"The American public is not interested in China."
- Rejection
It becomes the best-selling novel in the United States and wins The Pulitzer Prize. In 1938, Buck received the Nobel Prize for Literature.

Edgar Rice Burroughs (1875-1950) *Tarzan Of The Apes*
"We are returning your story, Tarzan of the Apes. We have given the work careful consideration and while interesting we find it does not fit in with our plans for the present year. Thanking you for submitting the story to us."
– Rejection Letter
Tarzan resulted in 25 sequels, countless adaptations and is among the most recognized literary characters ever created.

> RAND McNALLY & COMPANY
> THE RAND-McNALLY BUILDING
> CHICAGO
>
> August 20, 1913.
>
> Dear Sir:
>
> We are returning under separate cover The All-Story magazine (Oct.1912) containing your story, "Tarzan of the Apes."
> We have given the work careful consideration and while interesting we find it does not fit in with our plans for the present year.
> Thanking you for submitting the story to us, We are
>
> Yours very truly,
> Rand McNally & Co.
>
> Mr. Edgar Rice Burroughs,
>   2008 Park Avenue,
>   Chicago.

Edgar Rice Burroughs' *Tarzan* rejection letter, 1913.

Meg Cabot - *The Princess Diaries (2000)*
"NO!"
– Written and returned on Cabot's query letter
She endured two years of rejection, all of which she kept in a bag under her bed.
There are now over 25 million copies of her books in print.

Jack Canfield & Mark Victor Hansen – *Chicken Soup for the Soul Series*
"Anthologies don't sell."
– One of 140 Publisher's rejections
The series has sold more than 100 million copies.

Agatha Christie (1890-1976)
After years of rejection, Christie is paid £25 for her first novel.
She is now listed by the *Guinness Book of World Records* as the best-selling novelist of all time, with sales of four billion copies.

Mary Higgins Clark
"We found the heroine as boring as her husband did."
- Redbook Editor rejecting *Journey Back to Love*
Clark endured 6 years of rejection before first being published.
She has since sold more than 100 million copies of her books.
In 2000, she received a $64 million advance for her next five books.

Paulo Coelho *The Alchemist (1988)*
"It won't sell. You'll make more money in the stock exchange."
-Coelho's first publisher, cautioning him about its prospects
The book has sold more than 65 million copies in 56 languages.

E.E. Cummings – *No Thanks* (1935)
Rejected by 14 publishers, Cummings borrowed $300 from his mother
and changed the title from "*70 Poems*" to "*No Thanks.*"
The book was dedicated to all the publishers who had rejected it.

Patrick Dennis – *Auntie Mame (1955)*
Supposedly, he submitted in alphabetical order and all rejected it before Vanguard.
Mame spent 112 weeks on the bestseller list and sold more than 2 million copies.

Emily Dickinson (1830-1886)
Of the 1,800 or so poems she wrote, less than ten were published in her lifetime.
The few that were had to be changed to become more "suitable" for her era.
She's now known as one of the greatest American poets of all time.

William Faulkner (1897-1962)
"My chief objection is that you don't seem to have any story to tell and I contend that a novel should tell a story and tell it well."
- Rejection of *Flags in the Dust,* published as *Sartoris* (1929)

"Good God, I can't publish this. We'd both be in jail."
- Rejection letter for *Sanctuary* (1931)

Faulkner was awarded The Nobel Prize in Literature in 1949.
He also won The Pulitzer Prize for Fiction twice, in 1955 and 1963.

F. Scott Fitzgerald - (1896-1940) – *The Great Gatsby (1925)*
"You'd have a decent book if you'd get rid of that Gatsby character."
– Rejection letter

The Great Gatsby was published on April 10, 1925.
Fitzgerald cabled his editor, asking: *"Any news?"*
"Sales situation doubtful" was the reply.

Sales were indeed lousy and the reviews were mixed at best:
"Not the work of a wise and mature novelist."
"More than a little artificial, into the class of negligible novels."

Fitzgerald died in 1940, believing he had been a failure.
Gatsby is now consistently ranked among the greatest works of American literature.

Jasper Fforde - *The Eyre Affair (2001)*
He received 76 rejections before *The Eyre Affair* was published.
The book is now considered a classic of contemporary fantasy.

Gustave Flaubert (1821-1880) - *Madame Bovary (1856)*
*"You have buried your novel underneath a heap of details
which are well done but utterly superfluous."*
- Rejection letter

When printed in 1856, Flaubert was put on trial for obscenity.
He was acquitted in 1857.
The book is now considered a masterpiece.

Anne Frank (1929-1945) - *The Diary of Anne Frank (1947)*
*"The girl doesn't, it seems to me, have a special perception or feeling
which would lift that book above the 'curiosity' level."*
- One of 16 rejections.
Knopf rejected the U.S. rights after receiving this reader's report:
"Very dull...a dreary record of typical family bickering, petty annoyances and adolescent emotions. Even if the work had come to light five years ago, when the subject was timely, I don't see that there would have been a chance for it."
In 1952, Doubleday printed a modest run of 5,000 copies.
The diary has since been published in more than 60 languages.

"One of the wisest and most moving commentaries on war and its impact on human beings that I have ever read."
- Eleanor Roosevelt.

"Of all the multitudes who throughout history have spoken for human dignity in times of great suffering and loss, no voice is more compelling than that of Anne Frank."
- John F. Kennedy.

"On Robben Island, some of us read Anne Frank's Diary. We derived much encouragement from it. It kept our spirits high and reinforced our confidence in the invincibility of the cause of freedom and justice."
– Nelson Mandela

"Where there's hope, there's life. It fills us with fresh courage and makes us strong again."
– Anne Frank

William Golding - *The Lord Of The Flies (1954)*
"An absurd and uninteresting fantasy which was rubbish and dull."
- Early rejection letter
The book sold fewer than 3,000 copies when first released.
Eventually it became a best-seller and Golding won The Nobel Prize in Literature.

Kenneth Grahame - *The Wind In The Willows (1908)*
"An irresponsible holiday story that will never sell."
The book has become a classic of children's literature.
"I read it and reread it and have come to accept the characters as old friends."
– President Theodore Roosevelt (1909).

Zane Grey (1872-1939)
"You have no business being a writer and should give up."
- Early rejection
"The substance of any two Zane Grey books could be written upon the back of a postage stamp."
– Critic Heywood Broun.
He became one of the first millionaire authors and wrote more than 90 books.
In 1923, he penned a response to his critics:
"These critics who crucify me do not guess the littlest part of my sincerity. They must be burned in a blaze. I cannot learn from them."

John Grisham – *A Time To Kill (1989)*
16 literary agencies and 12 publishers rejected his first novel.
Eventually, a small publisher agreed to print 5,000 copies.
Grisham has now sold more than 275 million books worldwide.
"Life is much simpler ignoring reviews and the nasty people who write them. Critics should find meaningful work." – J.G.

Alex Haley - *Roots* (1976)

After ten years of research and rejections, *Roots* is published. The historical novel becomes an instant bestseller, eventually being published in 37 different languages, with the television series reaching 130 million viewers. In 1977, Haley received a special Pulitzer Prize for his work.

Joseph Heller - *Catch-22 (1961)*

"I haven't the foggiest idea about what the man is trying to say. Apparently the author intends it to be funny – possibly even satire – but it is really not funny on any intellectual level ... From your long publishing experience you will know that it is less disastrous to turn down a work of genius than to turn down talented mediocrities."
– Publisher's internal rejection memo

Catch-22 sold 10 million copies and the title became a part of the English language.

Ernest Hemingway (1899-1961)

"It would be extremely rotten taste, to say nothing of being horribly cruel, should we want to publish it."
- Rejection for *The Torrents of Spring* (1926).

"There is evidence of no mental growth whatever; there is no better understanding of life. Essentially, this new novel is an empty book. Mr. Hemingway's record as a creative writer would be stronger if it had never been published."
– The New York Times review of *To Have and Have Not* (1937).

Hemingway won The Pulitzer Prize in 1953 and The Nobel Prize in 1954.

75 Wiley Street
New York, N.Y.
U.S.A.

June 14th, 1925.

Dear Mr. Hemingway:

Thank you for sending us your manuscript, The Sun Also Rises. I regret to inform you that we will not be offering you publication at this time.
If I may be frank, Mr. Hemingway — you certainly are in your prose — I found your efforts to be both tedious and offensive. You really are a man's man, aren't you? I wouldn't be surprised to hear that you had penned this entire story locked up at the club, ink in one hand, brandy in the other. Your bombastic, dipsomaniac, where-to-now characters had me reaching for my own glass of brandy — something to liven up 250 pages of men who are constantly stopping to sleep off the drink. What Peacock & Peacock is looking for, in a manuscript, is innovation and heart. I'm afraid that what you have produced here does not fit that description.
A great story, Mr. Hemingway, is built on a foundation of great characters. I had trouble telling yours apart. Remind me, which is the broken-hearted bachelor who travels aimlessly across Europe? Ah, yes! They all do! As I understand it, Jake Barnes is intended to be your hero. A hero, Mr. Hemingway, is a person the reader can care about, root for. Jake Barnes is too detached, too ineffective; I doubt he'd have the energy to turn the page and find out what happened to himself. I take exception, also, to your portrayal of Mike. There is nothing less appealing than a character who sits blithely by while his wife sleeps with half of the continent. I have not yet said anything about Brett, your only prominent female character. As a woman, was I intended to identify with this flighty girl who takes in men the way the others take in after-supper coffees? Let me tell you, Mr. Hemingway, I did not. Your languid characters deserve each other, really each one is more hollow than the next.
Of course, I doubt it's possible to create a three-dimensional character with such two-dimensional language. Have you never heard of crafted prose? Style? Complexity of diction? It's hard to believe an entire novel's worth of pages could be filled up with the sort of short, stunted sentences you employ here. Let me be specific: at the start of the novel, you sum up a key character, Robert Cohn, with just five short words, "I was his tennis friend." This tells us nothing. Later, when Jake is looking out on the Seine — the beautiful, historic, poetic Sein — you write, "the river looked nice." Nice? The river looked nice? I dare say my young son could do better!
In short, your efforts have saddened me, Mr. Hemingway. I was hopeful that by 1925, the brutes would have stopped sending me their offerings. We at Peacock & Peacock, are looking to publish novels that will inspire. God knows, it's what people need at this time. Certainly, what is not needed are treatises about bullfights and underemployed men who drink too much.

Sincerely,
Mrs Moberley Luger

Frank Herbert (1920-1986) - *Dune (1965)*
"I might be making the mistake of the decade, but..."
- The opening line of 1 of 23 rejections.
Dune was eventually published by Chilton Books,
a small publisher typically known for printing auto repair manuals.
It became the best-selling science-fiction novel in history.

Thor Heyerdahl – *The Kon-Tiki Expedition (1948)*
"If no one drowned, the story isn't interesting."
"Long, solemn and tedious."
"Maybe a university press would buy it, but it's definitely not for us."
– 3 of the 20 rejections.
Kon-Tiki has since been translated into 71 languages and sold 20 million copies.

Tony Hillerman (1925-2008) – *The Navajo Novel Series*
"We suggest you get rid of all that Indian stuff."
- Rejection letter.
His *Navajo Tribal Police* books made him one of the richest people in New Mexico.

Khaled Hosseini, *The Kite Runner (2003)*
Hosseini initially wrote it as a short story, submitting to *Esquire* and *The New Yorker*. Both rejected it.
He came across the manuscript in his garage years later and expanded it into novel. It soon became a New York Times bestseller, with more than 7 million copies sold.

James Joyce, (1882-1941)
"Joyce revolutionized 20th century fiction."
- TIME Magazine, 1999.

Dubliners - (1914)
Written in 1905, *Dubliners* was rejected 21 times before being published in 1914.
379 copies sold in its first year, Joyce is believed to have bought 120 of them.

Portrait of the Artist as a Young Man - (1916)
"Rather discursive and the point of view is not an attractive one."
"It is not possible to get hold of an intelligent audience in wartime."
"A good bit of work but it won't pay."
- 3 early rejections
Later named third, on Modern Library's list of the 100 best English-language novels.

Ulysses - (1922)
When a portion was published in America in 1920, it led to an obscenity charge.
At the trial, the book was declared obscene and *Ulysses* was banned in the US.
The U.S. Post Office regularly burned the novel until the ban was lifted in 1933.
Ulysses has been called the greatest novel of the 20th century.

John Keats (1795-1821) – *Endymion (1818)*
"To witness the disease of any human understanding, however feeble, is distressing; but the spectacle of an able mind reduced to a state of insanity is of course ten times more afflicting. It is with such sorrow as this that we have contemplated the case of Mr. John Keats. The frenzy of the Poems was bad enough in its way; but it did not alarm us half so seriously as the calm, settled, imperturbable driveling idiocy of Endymion."
–John Gibson Lockhart, Blackwood's Magazine (1818).

"A thing of beauty is a joy for ever"
– The first line of *Endymion*.
Keats died at 25. He's one of the most beloved Romantic poets.

William Kennedy – *Ironweed (1983)*
"There is much about the novel that is very good and much that I did not like. When I throw in the balance the book's unrelenting lack of commerciality, I am afraid I just have to pass."
– Rejection.
Ironweed won The Pulitzer Prize for Fiction in 1984.

Jack Kerouac (1922-1969) - *On The Road* (1957)
"I don't dig this one at all."
– Internal Knopf rejection.

"This is a badly misdirected talent and this huge sprawling and inconclusive novel would probably have small sales and sardonic indignant reviews from every side."
– Internal Knopf rejection.

In 1951, this seminal novel was written in three weeks, on a single roll of paper. It took six years before it was finally published.

"It changed my life like it changed everyone else's."
– Bob Dylan.

Daniel Keyes (1927-2014) - *Flowers for Algernon (1959)*
"Dan, this is a good story, but I'm gonna tell you how to make it a great story: Charlie does not lose his intelligence; he remains a super-genius, and he and Alice fall in love, they get married, and live happily ever after."
- *Galaxy* editor Horace Gold (1958).

Keyes declined to change it and sold the short story elsewhere.
He later expanded it into a novel and tried to sell it to Doubleday,
who also wanted him to change the ending.
Keyes refused and returned Doubleday's advance.
Five more publishers rejected the story until Harcourt published the novel in 1966. It has since been widely translated and is taught in schools around the world.

Dennis Kimbro *Think and Grow Rich: A Black Choice (1992)*
"Rejection slips could wallpaper my room."
The book became a number 1 bestseller.

Stephen King – *Carrie (1974)*
"We are not interested in science fiction which deals with negative utopias. They do not sell."
– An early rejection.
King's first published novel *Carrie* began as a short story.
He wrote it while living with his wife Tabitha in a Maine trailer.
King wrote 3 pages then threw them away because he was disgusted with the idea.
His wife retrieved them from the garbage and encouraged him to finish.
He did, expanding it into a novel, which he sent to publishers.
Many rejected it before Doubleday editor William Thompson tried to contact him.
Because King couldn't afford a telephone, Thompson sent a telegram:
"Carrie Officially A Doubleday Book. $2,500 Advance Against Royalties. Congrats, Kid - The Future Lies Ahead, Bill."
The paperback rights soon sold for $400,000.
King has since sold more than 350 million copies of his books.

Rudyard Kipling, (1865-1936)
"I'm sorry Mr. Kipling, but you just don't know how to use the English language."
- San Francisco Examiner editor, firing him in 1889.
He became the first English language writer to receive The Nobel Prize in Literature.
He is still its youngest recipient.

John Knowles – *A Separate Peace (1958)*
"Embarrassingly overwrought...strikes me as much overdone and even pretentious. I feel rather hopeless about his having a future."
– Rejection letter.
In 1960, the book became a New York Times Bestseller.
In 1961, it was a finalist, with *To Kill A Mockingbird*, for The National Book Award.
Both lost.

Jerzy Kosiński (1933–1991) - *Steps* (1968)
*"A collection of unbelievably creepy little allegorical tableaux done in a terse elegant voice that's like nothing else anywhere ever.
Only Kafka's fragments get anywhere close to where Kosiński goes in this book, which is better than everything else he ever did combined."*
– David Foster Wallace.
Steps won the U.S. National Book Award for Fiction.

The *Steps* Experiment – (1975 & 1979)
(See also: The *Casablanca* Experiment)

As an experiment in 1975, writer Chuck Ross retyped the first 21 pages of *Steps* and sent it to 4 publishers (Random House, Houghton Mifflin, Doubleday, and Harcourt Brace Jovanovich), claiming it was a sample of his own work.

All of them rejected it, including the original publisher of *Steps*, Random House. When Ross revealed the experiment, Kosiński said that Ross should have retyped and sent the entire manuscript instead, saying:

"[Steps] depends very much on cumulative effect. I can see myself rejecting it...
It would have been much more interesting if he had submitted the whole work."

In 1979, Ross retyped the entire book and submitted it to 14 publishers including the original four, under a pseudonym.

All 14 rejected it.

Harcourt Brace Jovanovich, publisher of Kosiński's *Being There*, wrote:
"...the content of the book didn't inspire the level of enthusiasm here that a publisher should have for any book on their list in order to do well by it."

Houghton Mifflin, publisher of Kosiński's *The Painted Bird*, wrote:
"Several of us read your untitled novel here with admiration for the writing and style. Jerzy Kosiński comes to mind as a point of comparison when reading the stark, chilly episodic incidents you have set down. The drawback to the manuscript, as it stands, is that it doesn't add up to a satisfactory whole. It has some very impressive moments, but gives the impression of sketchiness and incompleteness."

Louis L'Amour (1908-1988)

Supposedly received 200 rejections before Bantam gave him a shot.
He has since sold 320 million copies of his books.

D.H. Lawrence - *Lady Chatterley's Lover* (1928)

"For your own good, do not publish this book."
– Rejection letter.

Censored or banned worldwide until the 1960's, when Penguin was acquitted of obscenity for publishing it, the book became a worldwide best-seller.

"It is most damnable! It is written by a man with a diseased mind and a soul so black that he would obscure even the darkness of hell!"
– U.S. Senator Reed Smoot, opposing lifting of ban (1930).

John le Carré - *The Spy Who Came in From the Cold* (1963)

"You are welcome to Le Carré, he hasn't got any future."
- Rejection letter

Publishers Weekly later called it the best spy novel of all-time.
More than 40 million copies have been sold.

Ursula K. Le Guin - *The Left Hand of Darkness* (1969)

"Hopelessly bogged down and unreadable."
- Rejection letter

It became an international bestseller and has been translated into 27 languages.

493 S. Larsson

På uppdrag av Samarbetsnämnden för Journalisthögskolorna kan vi härmed meddela Dig att Dina resultat på den skriftliga urvalsprövningen tyvärr ej varit tillräckliga i konkurrensen med övriga sökande. Du kan därför ej beredas plats vid Journalisthögskolorna hösten 1972.

Som tidigare meddelats har varje prövad möjlighet att erhålla mer ingående information om testresultaten. Från mitten av augusti kan sökanden bosatta i eller i närheten av Stockholm efter tidsbeställning komma upp till oss på institutet för personlig genomgång av testresultaten.

För sökande bosatta utanför Stockholm kommer delgivningssamtal att ordnas i Göteborg, Malmö och eventuellt Umeå i slutet av augusti. Har Du tillfälle och är intresserad av att ta del av Dina testresultat kan Du fylla i talongen nedan och skicka tillbaka den till oss före den 23 augusti. Du får då en kallelse till bestämd tid och plats.

Vår adress är: Psykotekniska institutet
Birger Jarlsgatan 22, 1½ tr.
114 34 STOCKHOLM

Rejection of Stieg Larsson. He later wrote *The Girl With The Dragon Tattoo/Millennium Trilogy*.

Dear Miss Kidd,

Ursula K. Le Guin writes extremely well, but I'm sorry to have to say that on the basis of that one highly distinguishing quality alone I cannot make you an offer for the novel. The book is so endlessly complicated by details of reference and information, the interim legends become so much of a nuisance despite their relevance, that the very action of the story seems to be to become hopelessly bogged down and the book, eventually, unreadable. The whole is so dry and airless, so lacking in pace, that whatever drama and excitement the novel might have had is entirely dissipated by what does seem, a great deal of the time, to be extraneous material. My thanks nonetheless for having thought of us. The manuscript of <u>The Left Hand of Darkness</u> is returned herewith. Yours sincerely,

The Editor

21 June, 1968

MARVEL COMICS GROUP
A DIVISION OF CADENCE
INDUSTRIES CORPORATION

Dear Mr. Lee,

Your work looks as if it were done by four different people. Your best pencils are on page 7, panel with agents (lower left corner), and close up of face. The rest of the pencils are of much weaker quality. The same can be said for your inking. Resubmit when your work is consistent and when you have learned to draw hands.

Best,

Eliot R. Brown

Eliot R. Brown
Submissions Editor

Jim Lee's rejection letter. He is currently Co-Publisher of DC Comics.

Madeleine L'Engle - *A Wrinkle in Time (1962)*
It was rejected by 26 publishers, possibly because, as L'Engle speculated:
"A Wrinkle in Time had a female protagonist in a science fiction book."
After failing to find a buyer, her agent returned the book to her.
By chance, L'Engle was introduced to John C. Farrar of Farrar, Straus and Giroux. They agreed to publish the book.
It won the 1963 Newbery Medal and has sold 8 million copies.

Jack London (1876-1916)
London's home museum displays many of his 600 rejections.
His first story sold was *To the Man On The Trail*, published in 1899.
The newspaper had promised him five dollars but was slow to pay.
London nearly quit writing until his story *A Thousand Deaths* sold for $40.
"I was at the end of my tether. Beaten out, starved...literally and literarily I was saved."
In 1903, he sold *The Call of the Wild* to The Saturday Evening Post for $750 and the book rights to Macmillan for $2,000.
He later became one of the first writers to receive worldwide acclaim and earn a comfortable living solely from his writing.

Robert Ludlum - *The Scarlatti Inheritance (1971)*
The first of his 27 thrillers was published after receiving many rejections.
Ludlum was later published in more than 30 languages with an estimated 290 million copies of his books in print, including the *Bourne* series.

Norman Maclean – *A River Runs Through It (1976)*
"These stories have trees in them."
– Part of a rejection letter.

Knopf rejected *A River Runs Through It,* before The University of Chicago published the book, to great success.

Years later, Maclean received a letter from Knopf, inquiring whether they might have a first look at his next book.

Maclean responded:

Dear Mr. Elliott:
    I have discovered that I have been writing you under false pretenses, although stealing from myself more than from you. I have stolen from myself the opportunity of seeing the dream of every rejected author come true.
    The dream of every rejected author must be to see, like sugar plums dancing in his head, please-can't-we-see-your-next-manuscript letters standing in piles on his desk, all coming from publishing companies that rejected his previous manuscript, especially from the more pompous of the fatted cows grazing contentedly in the publishing field. I am sure that, under the influence of those dreams, some of the finest fuck-you prose in the English language has been composed but, alas, never published. And to think that the rare moment in history came to me when I could in actuality have written the prose masterpiece for all rejected authors – and I didn't even see that history had swung wide its doors to me.
    You must have known that Alfred A. Knopf turned down my first collection of stories after playing games with it, or at least the game of cat's-paw, now rolling it over and saying they were going to publish it and then rolling it on its back when the president of the company announced it wouldn't sell. So I can't understand how you could ask if I'd submit my second manuscript to Alfred A. Knopf, unless you don't know my race of people. And I can't understand how it didn't register on me – 'Alfred A. Knopf' is clear enough on your stationery.
    But, although I let the big moment elude me, it has given rise to little pleasures. For instance, whenever I receive a statement of the sales of 'A River Runs Through It' from the University of Chicago Press, I see that someone has written across the bottom of it, 'Hurrah for Alfred A. Knopf.' However, having let the great moment slip by unrecognized and unadorned, I can now only weakly say this: if the situation ever arose when Alfred A. Knopf was the only publishing house remaining in the world and I was the sole remaining author, that would mark the end of the world of books.
Very sincerely,
Norman Maclean

Norman Mailer (1923-2007)
"This will set publishing back 25 years."
- Rejection for *The Deer Park (1955)*.

*"All other considerations which this book presents are subsidiary to the problem posed by the profanity and obscenity of its dialogue.
In my opinion it is barely publishable."*
-Bernard DeVoto advising rejection of *The Naked and The Dead*.

Mailer later won The Pulitzer Prize in Literature.
Twice.

Yann Martel - *Life of Pi (2001)*
At least 5 London publishers rejected the book.
It has since sold more than 10 million copies worldwide and won the prestigious Man Booker Prize for Fiction in 2002.

Peter Mathiessen- *Signs of Winter (unpublished)*
*"It is a very bad novel... There are a great many flashbacks and the thoughts of every character are reported faithfully ad nauseum. But since these people and their thoughts are adolescent, banal, self-pitying, trivial and totally unsympathetic, this conscientiousness merely adds to our dislike of "Signs of Winter."
We had great hopes for this guy on the basis of a few short stories but Matthiessen is still a painfully immature writer who needs to write a great deal more and a very patient editor.
Even so this does not seem salvageable to us
—let someone else struggle if they will. REJECT.
J.M. Fox - 3/16/53
I concur.
P. Vandrin - 3/16/53"*
- Rejection from Knopf Editors.
Matthiessen later received a National Book Award for Fiction.

W. Somerset Maugham– *The Razor's Edge (1944)*
"Not desirable. Much of the long discussion of the author's philosophy of life is tedious and the author's view pessimistic and hopeless. I do not think the book would have a large sale here and while I would not say that it is impossible, I think it is distasteful."
– Rejection letter.

Herman Melville (1819-1891) – *Moby Dick (1851)*
"First, we must ask, does it have to be a whale? While this is a rather delightful, if somewhat esoteric, plot device, we recommend an antagonist with a more popular visage among the younger readers. For instance, could not the Captain be struggling with a depravity towards young, perhaps voluptuous, maidens?"
– Rejection letter.
Only 3,215 copies sold in the last 40 years of Melville's life.

Reviews like this, didn't help:

"This is an ill-compounded mixture of romance and matter-of-fact. The style of his tale is in places disfigured by mad (rather than bad) English; and its catastrophe is hastily, weakly, and obscurely managed. We have little more to say in reprobation or in recommendation of this absurd book."
- London Athenaeum.

"Mr. Melville is evidently trying to ascertain how far the public will consent to be imposed upon. He is gauging, at once, our gullibility and our patience. Having written one or two passable extravagancies, he has considered himself privileged to produce as many more as he pleases, increasingly exaggerated and increasingly dull."
- U.S. Magazine and Democratic Review.

Moby Dick is now considered one of America's greatest novels.

Stephenie Meyer – *The Twilight Series (2005-2008)*

Meyer had no experience as a writer before writing *Twilight*.
On June 2, 2003, she had a dream which inspired the story.
By September 2003 she had turned her dream into a book.
She submitted her debut novel *Twilight* to 15 literary agencies.
5 failed to respond, 9 rejected it and 1 agreed to represent her.
In November 2003, six months after the dream, Meyer signed a three-book deal with Little, Brown & Co. for $750,000.
The first three books in the *Twilight* series have spent a combined 143 weeks on The New York Times Best Seller list.
The *Twilight* series has sold more than 100 million copies.
In 2009 she earned over $50 million and $40 million more in 2010.

Arthur Miller (1915-2005) - *Death of a Salesman* (1949)

"A man like Arthur Miller, he's got a gripe against certain phases of American life. I think he's done a lot of bad. Ours is a pretty good country and I don't think we ought to run it down. Sure there are fellows like Willy Loman, but you don't have to write plays about them."
– Gary Cooper (1956)

When producer Cheryl Crawford (who had a "first look" deal with Miller) read *Death of a Salesman*, she passed on it.
Several other prominent investors also backed out after reading it.
Many felt that the flashbacks would confuse an audience.
Miller consulted with his director Elia Kazan and Kazan's wife, both of whom agreed with the assessment, so he rewrote it.
When completed, few liked the rewrite any better. Producer Kermit Bloomgarden, who liked the original draft, said of the rewrite: *"This piece of shit, I will not do."*

Miller decided to revert back to the original and later said:
"I've done rewriting in early stages of various plays and on the whole, I regret what I did. There were some improvements, but you have to trade with things you've given away. My plays are structured and once you begin unraveling that structure, the whole mechanism begins to shudder. If it's going to fail, let it fail the way I wrote it, rather than the way I rewrote it."

A poll was taken and 98% of the respondents said they wouldn't see a play with the word "death" in the title, so the producers declared:
"The title is a disaster! Rename it Free and Clear."

Miller considered the change before Kazan helped convince him to keep the original. *Death of A Salesman* won The Pulitzer Prize for Drama in 1949.

L.M. Montgomery - *Anne of Green Gables (1908)*

She first wrote the novel in 1905 and sent it to five publishers, all of whom reject it. 3 years later, she resubmits and L.C. Page & Company agree to publish her debut. The novel has sold 50 million copies in 20 different languages.

Walter Mosley - *Devil in a Blue Dress (1990)*

"We already have a black detective." – Rejection letter.
Mosley has written forty books,
including ten starring his most popular character "Easy" Rawlins.

Alice Munro - *Dance of the Happy Shades (1968)*

"Nothing particularly new and exciting" and Munro is *"not that young."*
- Knopf editor Judith Jones' rejection letter.
Munro won the Man Booker International Prize in 2009 and
The Nobel Prize in Literature in 2013.

Vladimir Nabokov – *Lolita (1955)*

"Overwhelmingly nauseating, even to an enlightened Freudian. To the public, it will be revolting. The whole thing is an unsure cross between hideous reality and improbable fantasy. It often becomes a wild neurotic daydream. I recommend that it be buried under a stone for a thousand years."
- Rejection letter.

Rejected by Viking, Simon & Schuster, New Directions, Farrar, Straus, and Doubleday, the book is published in France in 1955. After the below review, *Lolita* is banned in the U.K.:
"The filthiest book I have ever read. Sheer unrestrained pornography."
– John Gordon, London Sunday Express

Now, the book is considered a masterpiece.

Audrey Niffenegger - *The Time Traveler's Wife (2003)*

25 literary agents rejected it before Niffenegger sent her debut novel to a small publisher in San Francisco, MacAdam/Cage.
It becomes a "publishing sensation" and Amazon's Book of the Year.
She received a $5 million advance for her second novel.

Catherine O'Flynn - *What Was Lost* (2007)
Her debut novel was rejected by 20 agents and publishers before being accepted by a small Birmingham, U.K. publisher.
It won the 2008 Costa Book Award.

George Orwell (1903-1950)
"Immature and unsatisfactory... I think, too that you deal with sex too much in your writings. Subjects a little less worldly would have a greater appeal!"
–Rejection for *The Sea God* (1929)

"It is decidedly too short."
– Rejection for *A Scullion's Diary,* later re-titled *Down and Out in Paris and London.*

"I regret to say that it does not appear to me possible as a publishing venture."
- Rejection by T.S. Eliot of Faber & Faber for *Down and Out in Paris and London.*

"It is impossible to sell animal stories in the U.S.A."
–Publisher's rejection for *Animal Farm.*

"Stupid & pointless fable in which the animals take over a farm and run it, and their society takes about the course of the Soviet Union as seen by Westbrook Pegler. It all goes to show that a parallel carried out to the last detail is boring and obvious. Even Pegler gets off a few smart lines now and then but this is damn dull. Very, very NFK."
(Not For Knopf).
– Knopf rejection for Animal Farm (1945)

"It would be less offensive if the predominant caste in the fable were not pigs. I think the choice of pigs as the ruling caste will no doubt give offense to many people, and particularly to anyone who is a bit touchy, as undoubtedly the Russians are."
– Publisher Jonathan Cape's rejection of *Animal Farm.*

13 July 1944

Dear Orwell,

I know that you wanted a quick decision about Animal Farm: but minimum is two directors' opinions, and that can't be done under a week. But for the importance of speed, I should have asked the Chairman to look at it as well. But the other director is in agreement with me on the main points. We agree that it is a distinguished piece of writing; that the fable is very skilfully handled, and that the narrative keeps one's interest on its own plane—and that is something very few authors have achieved since Gulliver.

On the other hand, we have no conviction (and I am sure none of other directors would have) that this is the right point of view from which to criticise the political situation at the present time. It is certainly the duty of any publishing firm which pretends to other interests and motives than mere commercial prosperity, to publish books which go against current of the moment: but in each instance that demands that at least one member of the firm should have the conviction that this is the thing that needs saying at the moment. I can't see any reason of prudence or caution to prevent anybody from publishing this book—if he believed in what it stands for.

Now I think my own dissatisfaction with this apologue is that the effect is simply one of negation. It ought to excite some sympathy with what the author wants, as well as sympathy with his objections to something: and the positive point of view, which I take to be generally Trotskyite, is not convincing. I think you split your vote, without getting any compensating stronger adhesion from either party—i.e. those who criticise Russian tendencies from the point of view of a purer communism, and those who, from a very different point of view, are alarmed about the future of small nations. And after all, your pigs are far more intelligent than the other animals, and therefore the best qualified to run the farm—in fact, there couldn't have been an Animal Farm at all without them: so that what was needed, (someone might argue), was not more communism but more public-spirited pigs.

I am very sorry, because whoever publishes this, will naturally have the opportunity of publishing your future work: and I have a regard for your work, because it is good writing of fundamental integrity.

Miss Sheldon will be sending you the script under separate cover.

Yours sincerely,
T. S. Eliot

Chuck Palahniuk

When he tried to have *Invisible Monsters* published, it was rejected for being *"too disturbing."* He wrote *Fight Club* as an attempt to disturb the publisher further.

Here's a review for *Diary* (2003) from Laura Miller at Salon:

"Imagine some crappy novels. Imagine that they're all written in the same phony, repetitive, bombastic style as this paragraph, all hopped-up imperatives and posturing one-liners. Imagine that they're sloppily put together.

Imagine that everything even remotely clever in them has been done before and better by someone else. Imagine that each one flaunts the kind of 'research' that can be achieved by leafing through a trade magazine for 30 minutes and is riddled with grating errors. Imagine that these books traffic in the half-baked nihilism of a stoned high school student who has just discovered Nietzsche and Nine-Inch Nails.

Does it hurt yet? Now, imagine that every five pages or so the author of these novels will describe something as smelling like shit or piss because the TRUTH is fucking ugly, man. Imagine that he affects to attack the shallow, simplistic, dehumanizing culture of commodity capitalism by writing shallow, simplistic, dehumanized fiction.

But, heck, why go to all the effort of imagining any of this when a new Chuck Palahniuk novel arrives at your local bookstore annually?"

- Laura Miller, Salon.

Here's Palahniuk's reply:

Dear Laura,
I have never responded to a review,
perhaps because I've never gotten such a cruel and mean-spirited one.
Please send me a copy of your latest book. I'd love to read it.
Until you can create something that captivates people, I'd invite you to just shut up. It's easy to attack and destroy an act of creation. It's a lot more difficult to perform one.
I'd also invite you to read the reviews Fitzgerald got for 'Gatsby'
from dull, sad, bitter people — like yourself.
– Chuck Palahniuk

James Patterson - *The Thomas Berryman Number (1976)*
More than 30 publishers rejected his debut novel.
It became a bestseller.
Berryman has since sold over 300 million copies of his books.

Laurence Peter - *The Peter Principle (1969)*
The book was reportedly rejected more than 20 times.
It became a number one bestseller.

Harold Pinter (1930-2008) - *The Birthday Party (1957)*
"My second play, The Birthday Party, I wrote in 1958 or 1957. It was totally destroyed by the critics of the day, who called it an absolute load of rubbish."
Its 1958 London debut provoked *"bewildered hysteria"* and closed after 8 performances, nearly derailing his career.
Pinter later won The Nobel Prize in Literature.

Robert M. Pirsig – *Zen and the Art of Motorcycle Maintenance (1974)*
The book is in The Guinness Book Of World Records for its 121 publisher rejections. It has sold more than 5 million copies and is considered a classic.

Sylvia Plath (1932-1963) – *The Bell Jar (1963)*

"Disappointing. Juvenile and overwrought."
– Rejection from Harper & Row.

Plath also submitted to Knopf, under the pseudonym "Victoria Lucas".
Below are the original in-house Knopf reviews:

[1] Reject recommended
"I'm not sure what Heinemann's sees in this first novel unless it is a kind of youthful American female brashness. But there certainly isn't enough genuine talent for us to take notice. - JBJ
[2] I have now re-read—or rather read more thoroughly—'The Bell Jar' with the knowledge that it is by Sylvia Plath which has added considerably to its interest for it is obviously flagrantly autobiographical. But it still is not much of a novel.
The trouble is that she has not succeeded in using her material in a novelistic way; there is no viewpoint, no sifting out of the experiences of being a Mademoiselle contest winner with the month in New York, the subsequent mental breakdown and suicide attempts, the brash loss of virginity at the end. One feels simply that Miss Plath is writing of them because things did happen to her and the incidents are in themselves good for a story, but throw them together and they don't necessarily add up to a novel. One never feels, for instance, the deep-rooted anguish that would drive this girl to suicide. It is too bad because Miss Plath has a way with words and a sharp eye or unusual and vivid detail. But maybe now that this book is out of her system she will use her talent more effectively next time. I doubt if anyone over here will pick this novel up, so we might well have a second chance."
– JBJ

Another Knopf reader also rejected *The Bell Jar*, less than 2 months after her suicide:

"RECOMMEND REJECTION
This is an ill-conceived, poorly written novel, and we would be doing neither ourselves nor the late Miss Plath any good service by offering it to the American public...
I don't doubt that certain elements of the British press will puff the book nicely, but Mrs. Jones's original four-line report strikes me as the only honest and responsible critical reaction to the work.
- P.G. 3/29/63"

Plath committed suicide in London on February 11, 1963;
a month after Heinemann had published *The Bell Jar* in the U.K.
She won The Pulitzer Prize in 1982.
The Bell Jar was her only novel.

THE NEW YORKER
No. 25 WEST 43rd STREET

EDITORIAL OFFICES
OXFORD 7-1414

November 7, 1962

Dear Miss Plath,

I'm sorry we decided against these poems. We like the second section of AMNESIAC very much, but cannot see any relation between it and the first section. Perhaps we're being dense. But would you think over the possibility of printing the second section alone under that title? If you would care to resubmit it that way, we'd be happy to consider it again.

Thank you for sending these poems to us, and we hope to see others.

Sincerely,

Howard Moss

Howard Moss

Miss Sylvia Plath
Court Green
North Tawton
Devonshire
England

Edgar Allen Poe (1809-1849)
"Readers in this country have a decided and strong preference for works in which a single and connected story occupies the entire volume."
- Rejection letter for his short story collection.
Poe was one of the first American short story writers and also among the first to attempt to earn a living purely as a writer.
Yeats called him *"vulgar"* and Ralph Waldo Emerson said of The Raven:
"I see nothing in it."
He essentially invented the detective fiction genre.
"Where was the detective story until Poe breathed the breath of life into it?"
- Sir Arthur Conan Doyle.
Poe is now known as one of the most important American writers in history and his work influenced countless others.
He died at age 40.
His last words were: *"Lord help my poor soul."*

Beatrix Potter - *The Tale of Peter Rabbit (1901)*
Peter Rabbit was rejected by every publisher Potter tried, so she self-published the book, printing 250 copies.
It has since sold 45 million copies and been translated into 36 languages.

Ezra Pound - *Portrait D'une Femme (1912)*
"The opening line contains too many 'r's."
- Rejection
The poem's opening line is:
"Your mind and you are our Sargasso Sea"

Hugh Prather - *Notes To Myself (1970)*
After two years of rejection as a writer, a small, husband and wife publisher with only 3 prior books and no east coast distribution, accepts the book.
It becomes a bestseller, with more than 5 million copies sold.

Marcel Proust - *Remembrance of Things Past (1913-1927)*
"I may be dead from the neck up, but rack my brains as I may I can't see why a chap should need thirty pages to describe how he turns over in bed before going to sleep."
- Rejection letter.
After the 4000 page handwritten book had been rejected by leading publishers, Proust paid for the first printing himself.
It has become one of the most critically acclaimed works of fiction ever created.

Ayn Rand (1905-1982)
Rejections for *The Fountainhead (1943)*:
"It is badly written and the hero is unsympathetic."
"It is too intellectual for a novel."

"This is a work of almost genius – genius in the power of its expression- almost in the sense of its enormous bitterness. I wish there were an audience for a book of this kind. But there isn't. It wont sell."

Rejection for *Atlas shrugged (1957)*:
*"The book is much too long. There are too many long speeches...
I regret to say that the book is unsaleable and unpublishable."*

Both *The Fountainhead* and *Atlas shrugged* became bestsellers.

Henry Roth - *Call It Sleep (1934)*
"As a practical commercial venture, I am against it."
– Rejection.
The book sold poorly when published and went out of print for 30 years.
It was revived when reviewed on the front page of The New York Times Book Review in 1964 and the paperback edition sold over a million copies.

Philip Roth - *Portnoy's Complaint (1969)*
The book was "*a prohibited import*" in Australia and many libraries in the U.S. banned it because of the explicit language and candid discussion of masturbation.
Roth later commented about being a writer:
"Don't judge it. Just write it. It's not for you to judge it."

J.K Rowling – *The Harry Potter series (1997-2007)*
Rowling was a depressed single mother living on welfare who had considered suicide when she began writing *Harry Potter*.
She sent the book to several agents and one agreed to represent her.
Her agent then submitted the book to nine publishers. Eight rejected it.
The 9th only agreed to publish it after the 8-year-old daughter of the chairman read the first chapter and provided a glowing review to her father.
Rowling received a £2,500 advance for *Harry Potter*.
It was suggested that she change her name for publication from Joanne to something more "gender neutral". The books have sold 450 million copies and been translated into 70 languages.
Rowling briefly became a billionaire, before donating nearly $200 million to charity.
In a 2008 Harvard commencement speech, she said:
*"... You might never fail on the scale I did, but some failure in life is inevitable.
It is impossible to live without failing at something, unless you live so cautiously that you might as well not have lived at all – in which case, you fail by default...
You will never truly know yourself, or the strength of your relationships,
until both have been tested by adversity."*

J.D. Salinger (1919-2010) - *The Catcher In The Rye (1951)*
"The kid is disturbed."
– Rejection

"I had to show it to the textbook department. It's about a kid in prep school, isn't it? I'm waiting for their reply."
- Eugene Reynal, Harcourt, Brace & Co.

"This book is not for us, try Random House."
– Harcourt, Brace & Co. textbook department's reply.

"Too precocious, clever and showoffy"
- The New Yorker, declining to run an excerpt.

The Catcher in the Rye has sold 65 million copies.
It has been published in nearly all of the world's major languages.

Charles Schulz (1922-2000) – *Peanuts (1950-2000)*
All of his drawings were rejected by his high-school yearbook.
60 years later, a Snoopy statue was placed in their main office.
He was rejected for a cartoonist job at Walt Disney Studios.
Schulz later became one of the most popular and influential cartoonists in history.
*"In countless ways, Schulz blazed the wide trail
that most every cartoonist since has tried to follow."*
- Bill Watterson (2007).

Theodor Seuss Geisel a.k.a. Dr. Seuss (1904-1991)
And to Think That I Saw It on Mulberry Street (1937)
"Too different from other juveniles on the market to warrant its selling."
– Rejection letter.
At least 20 publishers rejected Geisel's first book.
Shortly after receiving his latest rejection, he was walking home
"*To burn the manuscript*" when he bumped into into a former Dartmouth schoolmate who had become a children's book editor.
Dr. Seuss has since sold several hundred million copies of his books.

George Bernard Shaw (1856-1950)
*"A novel of a most disagreeable kind. The thought of the book is all wrong;
the whole idea of it is odd, perverse and crude.
It is the work of a man writing about life, when he knows nothing of it."*
- Rejection for *The Irrational Knot (1905)* (written in 1880).

*"He will never be popular in the usual sense of the word and
perhaps scarcely remunerative."*
– Rejection for *Man and Superman* (1905)
Shaw became the only person to have been awarded a Nobel Prize and an Oscar®.

Mary Shelley (1797-1851) - *Frankenstein (1818)*

In 1816, 18 year-old Mary Wollstonecraft Godwin, daughter of prominent feminist Mary Wollstonecraft and future wife of Romantic poet Percy Shelley, wrote Frankenstein on a dare. Rejected by most publishers, Mary persuades a small London company to print 500 copies anonymously in 1818.

Reviews were harsh:

"A tissue of horrible and disgusting absurdity."

The book became a classic.

Shel Silverstein (1930-1999) - *The Giving Tree (1964)*

"Look, Shel, the trouble with this Giving Tree of yours is that it's not a kid's book - too sad, and it isn't for adults - too simple."

- William Cole, Simon & Schuster

"That tree is sick! Neurotic!"

- Harper & Row editor, recommending rejection.

Fortunately, Harper & Row's Ursula Nordstrom, who once said: *"I publish good books for bad children"* discovered the book and became Silverstein's (along with Maurice Sendak's) editor.

Translated into more than 30 languages, Silverstein's books have sold over 20 million copies. He also wrote Johnny Cash's *"A Boy Named Sue"*.

Upton Sinclair (1878-1968) - *The Jungle (1906)*

"The improbabilities are so glaring that even a boy reader would balk at them. It is fit only for the wastebasket." – Rejection.

"I advise without hesitation and unreservedly against the publication of this book which is gloom and horror unrelieved. One feels that what is at the bottom of his fierceness is not nearly so much desire to help the poor as hatred of the rich."

- Macmillan rejection.

After many rejections, Sinclair paid for the first printing himself. Doubleday later published an abridged version in 1906. The book galvanized public support for government legislation and regulation of the meat industry.

He won a Pulitzer Prize in 1943.

Isaac Bashevis Singer (1902-1991) - *Satan in Goray (1955)*

"It's Poland and the rich Jews again. I honestly do not think it worth Knopf's time and effort, though I do think that Spiegel will persist until he gets someone to publish. Personally, I'd reject."

- Knopf reader "H.W." (4/9/59)

Singer's first published work later became a bestseller.

In 1978, he won The Nobel Prize in Literature.

Nicholas Sparks - *The Notebook (1996)*

24 literary agencies had rejected Sparks' first novel before literary agent Theresa Park "discovered" him by picking the manuscript out of her agency's slush pile.
It sold in one week to Time Warner for $1 million.

Garth Stein - *The Art Of Racing In The Rain (2008)*

"It's narrated by a dog. No one will buy it. Write another one."
- Stein's (former) agent.
He fires her and gets new representation.
The novel ends up on the New York Times bestseller list for 156 weeks.

FROM ARTHUR C. FIFIELD, PUBLISHER,
13, CLIFFORD'S INN, LONDON, E.C.
TELEPHONE 14430 CENTRAL.

April 19 1912.

Dear Madam,

I am only one, only one, only one. Only one being, one at the same time. Not two, not three, only one. Only one life to live, only sixty minutes in one hour. Only one pair of eyes. Only one brain. Only one being. Being only one, having only one pair of eyes, having only one time, having only one life, I cannot read your M.S. three or four times. Not even one time. Only one look, only one look is enough. Hardly one copy would sell here. Hardly one. Hardly one.

Many thanks. I am returning the M.S. by registered post. Only one M.S. by one post.

Sincerely yours,

A. Fifield

Miss Gertrude Stein,
27 Rue de Fleurus,
Paris,
France.

Gertrude Stein's rejection letter

John Steinbeck (1902-1968)
"...for its unflattering portrayal of area residents."
– Explanation for the banning of *The Grapes Of Wrath (1939)*.

"Promoting euthanasia, condoning racial slurs, anti-business, containing profanity, containing vulgar and offensive language."
- Explanations given for banning *Of Mice and Men (1937)*.

Both still regularly appear on "Most Challenged Books" lists.
The Grapes Of Wrath won The Pulitzer Prize in 1940.
Steinbeck won the Nobel Prize for Literature in 1962.

Kathryn Stockett - *The Help (2009)*
"There is no market for this kind of tiring writing."
- Rejection from an agent.
Stockett received 60 rejections for her first novel.
"After my five years of writing and three and a half years of rejection, an agent named Susan Ramer took pity on me. What if I had given up at 15? Or 40? Or even 60?"
The book sold over five million copies and spent more than 100 weeks on
The New York Times Best Seller list.

Irving Stone (1903-1989) - *Lust For Life (1934)*
"A long, dull novel about an artist."
- Publisher's rejection.
When published, the book about van Gogh sells 25 million copies
and is the basis for a 1956 Oscar® winning film.

Jacqueline Susann - *Valley of the Dolls (1966)*
"She is a painfully dull, inept, clumsy, undisciplined, rambling and thoroughly amateurish writer whose every sentence, paragraph and scene cries for the hand of a pro. She wastes endless pages on utter trivia, writes wide-eyed romantic scenes that would not make the back pages of True Confessions, hauls out every terrible show biz cliché in all the books, lets every good scene fall apart and allows her book to ramble aimlessly...most of the first 200 pages are virtually worthless and dreadfully dull and practically every scene is dragged out flat and stomped on by her endless talk."
– Rejection.
It became the bestselling book of 1966 and has sold more than 30 million copies.

Henry David Thoreau (1817-1862) - *Walden (1852)*
"Womanish...un-manly...almost dastardly."
– Robert Louis Stevenson.
It took Thoreau eight drafts over ten years to write *Walden*.
Only 2,000 copies were sold in the five years after publication.
It is now considered one of America's greatest books.

John Kennedy Toole (1937-1969) - *A Confederacy Of Dunces*
"Obsessively foul and grotesque."
– Rejection letter.

"Ken" Toole's magnum opus has a tragic history.
He started writing it in 1963 while stationed at an army base in Puerto Rico
finishing in 1964 at his childhood home in New Orleans.
He sent the book to several publishers including Simon & Schuster,
where it found its way to noted editor Robert Gottlieb.
Gottlieb felt the book had a "*major problem*" which required a complete rewrite.
In December 1964, he wrote to Toole:
*"The book...does not have a reason; it's a brilliant exercise in invention,
but it isn't really about anything. And that's something no one can do anything about."*

Toole later spoke by phone with Gottlieb, who suggested
he discard *Dunces* and focus on writing a new book instead.
Toole was shattered.
His mother convinced him to take the book to publisher Hodding Carter Jr.
Carter showed no interest.
Humiliated at his failures, Toole grew increasingly despondent and erratic while *Dunces*
gathered dust in his childhood bedroom.
On March 26, 1969, he killed himself.

After his suicide, his mother made it her mission to find a publisher for the book,
believing it would vindicate her son.
She sent the manuscript to publishers over the next 5 years and it was rejected.
In 1976, she repeatedly pestered author Walker Percy to read the book.
He ignored her until she finally barged into his office, demanding that he read it.
As Percy later wrote:

*"The lady was persistent, and it somehow came to pass that she stood in my office handing
me the hefty manuscript. There was no getting out of it;
only one hope remained—that I could read a few pages and that they would be bad enough
for me, in good conscience, to read no farther.
Usually I can do just that. Indeed the first paragraph often suffices.
My only fear was that this one might not be bad enough, or might be just good enough,
so that I would have to keep reading.
In this case I read on. And on. First with the sinking feeling that it was not bad enough to
quit, then with a prickle of interest, then a growing excitement,
and finally an incredulity: surely it was not possible that it was so good."*

Even with Percy's endorsement, it took three more years before
Louisiana State University Press agreed to print *Dunces*.
The published version was Toole's largely unrevised first draft.
In 1981, twelve years after his suicide,
Toole was awarded The Pulitzer Prize for Fiction for *A Confederacy of Dunces*.

Alice Walker – *The Color Purple (1982)*
In 1980, Little, Brown & Company rejected a book deal with Ms. Walker.
The Color Purple won The Pulitzer Prize in 1983.

Jason Wallace - *Out of Shadows (2010)*
99 literary agents rejected the book, or failed to respond at all.
When published, it wins the Costa Children's Book Award.

H.G. Wells (1866-1946)
"It is not interesting enough for the general reader and not thorough enough for the scientific reader."
- Rejection for *The Time Machine (1895)*.

"An endless nightmare. I do not think it would take...
I think the verdict would be 'Oh, don't read that horrid book.'"
– Rejection for *The War Of The Worlds* (1898).

"...Only a minor writer of no large promise."
- Rejection for *Mankind in the Making (1903)*.

Wells is now often referred to as the father of science fiction.

Walt Whitman - *Leaves Of Grass (1855)*
"A mass of stupid filth"
-Rufus Wilmot Griswold, *The Criterion*, November 10, 1855

"It is no discredit to Walt Whitman that he wrote Leaves of Grass,
only that he did not burn it afterwards."
–Thomas Wentworth Higginson, *The Atlantic*, 1867

"The book cannot attain to any very wide influence."
–*The Atlantic, January 1882*

Whitman finally published *Leaves of Grass* with his own money.
He became one of the most influential poets in the America.

E.B. White (1899-1985)
"I was never so disappointed in a book in my life."
- Reviewer Anne Moore, re; *Stuart Little* (1945).

Moore wrote to White, his wife and his editor, advising against publication because: *"It lacked realistic fantasy, the character development was labored and the illustrations were out of scale."*

When White's editors at Harper's read *Charlotte's Web* (1952) before publication, they requested that he "*soften*" the ending.
White refused.
Both books are now considered classics of children's literature.

Oscar Wilde (1854-1900)
"To live is the rarest thing in the world. Most people exist, that is all."

"It contains unpleasant elements."
- Rejection for *The Picture of Dorian Gray* (1891).

"My dear sir, I have read your manuscript. Oh, my dear sir."
- Rejection for *Lady Windermere's Fan* (1892).

Oscar Wilde was a novelist, poet and playwright, who encountered scorn, derision and rejection for some of his works and all of his lifestyle. Tried several times for "gross indecency", he was convicted and sentenced to prison. He died at age 46 in Paris, largely because of ill-health related to his imprisonment.

"When first I was put into prison some people advised me to try and forget who I was. It was ruinous advice.
It is only by realising what I am that I have found comfort of any kind.
Now I am advised by others to try on my release to forget that I have ever been in a prison at all. I know that would be equally fatal.
It would mean that I would always be haunted by an intolerable sense of disgrace, and that those things that are meant for me as much as for anybody else –
the beauty of the sun and moon, the pageant of the seasons, the music of daybreak and the silence of great nights, the rain falling through the leaves,
or the dew creeping over the grass and making it silver –
would all be tainted for me, and lose their healing power,
and their power of communicating joy.
To regret one's own experiences is to arrest one's own development.
To deny one's own experiences is to put a lie into the lips of one's own life.
It is no less than a denial of the soul."
- Oscar Wilde, *De Profundis* (1897)

Thomas Wolfe - *Look Homeward, Angel (1929)*
"Terrible."
– A one-word rejection letter for Wolfe's first novel.

William P. Young - *The Shack (2007)*
After being rejected by 26 publishers, Young self-publishes the book.
It sells over 10 million copies and spent 70 weeks as a New York Times Best Seller.

PRO TIPS

"A good play is an act of aggression against the status quo."
- Edward Albee

"I discovered that rejections are not altogether a bad thing. They teach a writer to rely on his own judgment and to say in his heart of hearts, 'To hell with you.'"
– Saul Bellow

"One should fight like the devil the temptation to think well of editors...by the nature of their profession they read too much, with the result they grow jaded and cannot recognize talent though it dances in front of their eyes."
– John Gardner

"You don't want to dwell on your enemies, you know. I basically feel so superior to my critics for the simple reason that they haven't done what I do.
Most book reviewers haven't written 11 novels. Many of them haven't written one."
- John Irving

"Talent is cheaper than table salt.
What separates the talented individual from the successful one is a lot of hard work."
- Stephen King

"I would advise anyone who aspires to a writing career that before developing his talent he would be wise to develop a thick hide."
- Harper Lee

"[My writing] has stopped; I don't have any energy anymore.
This is why I keep telling anyone younger than me, don't imagine you'll have it forever. Use it while you've got it because it'll go; it's sliding away like water down a plug hole."
- Doris Lessing

"I write books that seem more suitable for children, and that's OK with me.
They are a better audience and tougher critics.
Kids tell you what they think, not what they think they should think."
- Maurice Sendak

"Any reviewer who expresses rage and loathing for a novel is preposterous.
He or she is like a person who has put on full armor and attacked a hot fudge sundae."
- Kurt Vonnegut

"Literature is strewn with the wreckage of men
who have minded beyond reason the opinions of others."
- Virginia Woolf

The Takeaway

Several persistent themes emerged as I researched this project.

One: *Times change.*
When critics went apeshit over the Impressionists or Lolita was banned as obscene, although it wasn't that long ago, the world was a *very* different place.
Less than a hundred years ago, *women couldn't vote in the United States.*
Fifty years ago, *African Americans couldn't go to the same schools as whites.*
Naturally, this begs the question: What are we outraged about today, that people will look back on in 50 years and say: "What a bunch of provincial crybabies"?

Here's an old-timey picture to help illustrate my point:

Washington policeman Bill Norton measuring the distance between knee and suit at the Tidal Basin bathing beach after Col. Sherrell, Superintendent of Public Buildings and Grounds, issued an order that suits not be over six inches above the knee. 6/30/22 - National Photo Co.

Two: *A Sense of Purpose.*
I was surprised to learn that several of these giants of history, battled depression. It seems that many (MLK, Lincoln, Churchill, etc.) kept it at bay or even flourished, when they had a cause or some sort of "higher calling" to focus their energies on.

Three: *Perseverance.*
There always seems to be someone (often more than just one) who outright rejects, or endeavors in some way to interfere with the pursuit of a dream.
Frequently they'll appear as "gatekeepers" or well-intentioned friends, even family.
Often it's the creator's themselves, sabotaging their own work through self-doubt.
Either way, these corrosive elements consistently seem to show up.

The takeaway here appears to be: believe in yourself, even when no one else does.
I was particularly heartbroken to learn that Ken Toole, van Gogh and several others, killed themselves before acclaim found them. I'm very grateful that for the most part, the people in this book persevered despite frequent rejection.

I suspect history is littered with enormously gifted talents who we will never know about... because they gave up.
Imagine if the Impressionists *had* quit, or Elvis *had* gone back to driving a truck?
The world would be a much duller place.

Four: *Chance.*
I think the luck component is undeniable (but one must first do the work).
I was amazed to learn Dr. Seuss was so demoralized by rejection that he was on his way home *to burn his first book*(!) when a chance encounter with an old friend, changed history.

Five: *Encouragement.*
What if Tabitha King <u>hadn't</u> rescued the first 3 pages of *Carrie* from the trash and convinced Stephen to finish? So, if you or someone you care about has a dream, *whatever it may be*? Support, buoy and embolden them... or yourself.

Six: *Influence.*
I'm not a huge fan of Kerouac's *On The Road* but I am a huge fan of Bob Dylan, Hunter S. Thompson and the countless others who were likely influenced by it.
Point being: you never know how your efforts may affect or inspire someone else.

So, bottom line:
Please start or continue to follow your heart, wherever it leads.

And one more thing:
Not *if*, but *when* you get rejected?
Here's <u>my</u> Pro Tip:

Ready?

"Fuck 'em."

Robert Lawton - near Yosemite, California.
November 15, 2014.

Acknowledgements

I ended up going down some fascinating rabbit holes while researching this project.
I encourage you to Google anything or anyone in here that appeals to you.
I bet you'll be thrilled and amazed at how far you wind up from where you started.

Here's a cool jumping off point:
Go listen to Elvis, on the evening of July 5, 1954, singing *That's All Right*.
It's pretty stunning.

Also:
I came across a lot of dubious information while researching this book.
A few of many examples:

Jimmy Denny, manager of The Grand Ole Opry is often cited as the source of the *"You ought to go back to drivin' a truck"* Elvis, quote.
From the best I can tell, it wasn't him at all, but Eddie Bond.

"Everything that can be invented has been invented"
- Charles H. Duell, Comissioner of the US Patent Office, 1899.
This appears to be a completely bogus quote.

"You'd better learn secretarial work or else get married."
Supposedly, this was said to Marilyn Monroe by Emmeline Snively in 1944.
Great quote. Problem is, Marilyn didn't show up at her modeling agency until August, 1945 and Snively claims to have been an early champion of Marilyn's from jump, so...
while it may be true, it's unverifiable.

There are tons of these floating around and I performed best efforts to fact check. That said, there may be errors, so please let me know if I screwed up & I'll fix it.

Much personal gratitude must be expressed to:
Ed Begley Jr., Brad Frazer at Hawley, Troxell, David Greenman, K. Kay Mercein Mann, Erick Schiele, Matt Shatz, Barry Teitelbaum, Cliff Weber at Spruce Law Group, Billy Wirth, my beloved dogs and my family.

These are by no means comprehensive lists.
I was constrained by my own taste preferences and frequent faults of memory.
No disrespect intended to the many great artists absent from here.

NOTES

Fred Astaire. (2014, September 18). In *Wikipedia, The Free Encyclopedia*. Retrieved 16:44, September 21, 2014, from
http://en.wikipedia.org/w/index.php?title=Fred_Astaire&oldid=626077887

http://armoryshow.si.edu/

http://www.newyorker.com/magazine/1963/04/06/the-armory-show-revolution-reenacted

http://ucblibrary3.berkeley.edu/goldman/Curricula/ArtLiterature/armoryshow.html

Armory Show. (2014, September 3). In *Wikipedia, The Free Encyclopedia*. Retrieved 16:04, September 21, 2014, from
http://en.wikipedia.org/w/index.php?title=Armory_Show&oldid=623989547

http://www.vulture.com/2013/02/saltz-revisits-1913-armory-show.html

"Matisse Souvenir de Biskra". Via Wikipedia -
http://en.wikipedia.org/wiki/File:Matisse_Souvenir_de_Biskra.jpg#mediaviewer/File:Matisse_Souvenir_de_Biskra.jpg

http://armory.nyhistory.org/matisse-burns-in-chicago/

Francis Bacon (artist). (2014, September 19). In *Wikipedia, The Free Encyclopedia*. Retrieved 16:08, September 21, 2014, from
http://en.wikipedia.org/w/index.php?title=Francis_Bacon_(artist)&oldid=626197085

http://topics.nytimes.com/top/reference/timestopics/people/b/francis_bacon/index.html?inline=nyt-per

Painting (1946). (2014, July 3). In *Wikipedia, The Free Encyclopedia*. Retrieved 16:08, September 21, 2014, from
http://en.wikipedia.org/w/index.php?title=Painting_(1946)&oldid=615407341

http://www.cnn.com/2013/11/12/us/francis-bacon-painting-art-auction/

"Painting 1946". Via Wikipedia -
http://en.wikipedia.org/wiki/File:Painting_1946.jpg#mediaviewer/File:Painting_1946.jpg

http://www.musee-orsay.fr/en/collections/works-in-focus/painting/commentaire_id/a-modern-olympia-

20442.html?S=1&cHash=d1a9f1fa1c&tx_commentaire_pi1%5Bfrom%5D=841&tx_commentaire_pi1%5BpidLi%5D=509&print=1&no_cache=1&

http://books.google.com/books?id=POnwVSI3KxMC&pg=PA32&lpg=PA32&dq=cezanne+delirium+tremens&source=bl&ots=oh8Py7HlK_&sig=GttdXYDBHeriDcdeVaHrBjFrZdU&hl=en&sa=X&ei=GhAbVLrnJJbqoATowYGIDQ&ved=0CCYQ6AEwAQ#v=onepage&q=cezanne%20delirium%20tremens&f=false

http://news.google.com/newspapers?nid=1499&dat=19600701&id=yPApAAAAIBAJ&sjid=6iUEAAAAIBAJ&pg=4700,56316

Paul Cézanne. (2014, September 17). In *Wikipedia, The Free Encyclopedia*. Retrieved 16:10, September 21, 2014, from http://en.wikipedia.org/w/index.php?title=Paul_C%C3%A9zanne&oldid=625924655

The Card Players. (2014, August 4). In *Wikipedia, The Free Encyclopedia*. Retrieved 16:11, September 21, 2014, from http://en.wikipedia.org/w/index.php?title=The_Card_Players&oldid=619790383

http://www.vanityfair.com/culture/2012/02/qatar-buys-cezanne-card-players-201202

"Card Players-Paul Cezanne" by Paul Cézanne - http://www.the-athenaeum.org/art/full.php?ID=6371. Licensed under Public domain via Wikimedia Commons - http://commons.wikimedia.org/wiki/File:Card_Players-Paul_Cezanne.jpg#mediaviewer/File:Card_Players-Paul_Cezanne.jpg

http://www.biographyonline.net/artists/paul-cezanne.html

http://www.philamuseum.org/collections/permanent/51449.html

Nude Descending a Staircase, No. 2. (2014, September 2). In *Wikipedia, The Free Encyclopedia*. Retrieved 16:12, September 21, 2014, from http://en.wikipedia.org/w/index.php?title=Nude_Descending_a_Staircase,_No._2&oldid=623878165

"Duchamp - Nude Descending a Staircase". Via Wikipedia - http://en.wikipedia.org/wiki/File:Duchamp_-_Nude_Descending_a_Staircase.jpg#mediaviewer/File:Duchamp_-_Nude_Descending_a_Staircase.jpg

http://www.juilliard.edu/journal/1402/armory-show

http://www.npr.org/2013/02/17/172002686/armory-show-that-shocked-america-in-1913-celebrates-100

Paul Gauguin. (2014, September 3). In *Wikipedia, The Free Encyclopedia*. Retrieved 16:14, September 21, 2014, from
http://en.wikipedia.org/w/index.php?title=Paul_Gauguin&oldid=623970225

http://www.telegraph.co.uk/culture/art/art-features/8008715/Paul-Gauguin-at-the-Tate-Modern-desire-death-myth.html

"Paul Gauguin - Deux Tahitiennes" by Paul Gauguin. Licensed under Public domain via Wikimedia Commons - http://commons.wikimedia.org/wiki/File:Paul_Gauguin_-_Deux_Tahitiennes.jpg#mediaviewer/File:Paul_Gauguin_-_Deux_Tahitiennes.jpg

"Tropical Vegetation" by Paul Gauguin - Pic. Licensed under Public domain via Wikimedia Commons -
http://commons.wikimedia.org/wiki/File:Tropical_Vegetation.jpg#mediaviewer/File:Tropical_Vegetation.jpg

Impressionism. (2014, September 15). In *Wikipedia, The Free Encyclopedia*. Retrieved 16:15, September 21, 2014, from
http://en.wikipedia.org/w/index.php?title=Impressionism&oldid=625700553

http://www.artchive.com/galleries/1874/74leroy.htm

http://www.impressionism.org/teachimpress/browse/aboutimpress.htm

http://arthistory.about.com/od/impressionism/a/impressionism_10one.htm

Impression, Sunrise. (2014, August 29). In *Wikipedia, The Free Encyclopedia*. Retrieved 16:16, September 21, 2014, from
http://en.wikipedia.org/w/index.php?title=Impression,_Sunrise&oldid=623363778

"Claude Monet, Impression, soleil levant" by Claude Monet - wartburg.edu. Licensed under Public domain via Wikimedia Commons - http://commons.wikimedia.org/wiki/File:Claude_Monet,_Impression,_soleil_levant.jpg#mediaviewer/File:Claude_Monet,_Impression,_soleil_levant.jpg

http://www.artchive.com/galleries/1874/74leroy.htm

http://mentalfloss.com/article/30497/11-early-scathing-reviews-works-now-considered-masterpieces

http://painting.about.com/library/biographies/blartistquotesimpressionists.htm

Gustav Klimt. (2014, September 16). In *Wikipedia, The Free Encyclopedia*. Retrieved 16:17, September 21, 2014, from
http://en.wikipedia.org/w/index.php?title=Gustav_Klimt&oldid=625862857

"Gustav Klimt 046" by Gustav Klimt - http://www.neuegalerie.org/collection/Austrian/Fine%20Arts?page=1. Licensed under Public domain via Wikimedia Commons - http://commons.wikimedia.org/wiki/File:Gustav_Klimt_046.jpg#mediaviewer/File:Gustav_Klimt_046.jpg

Édouard Manet. (2014, September 2). In *Wikipedia, The Free Encyclopedia*. Retrieved 16:18, September 21, 2014, from http://en.wikipedia.org/w/index.php?title=%C3%89douard_Manet&oldid=623790546

http://www.salon.com/2002/05/13/olympia_2/

"Edouard Manet - Luncheon on the Grass - Google Art Project" by Édouard Manet - twELHYoc3ID_VA at Google Cultural Institute, zoom level maximum. Licensed under Public domain via Wikimedia Commons - http://commons.wikimedia.org/wiki/File:Edouard_Manet_-_Luncheon_on_the_Grass_-_Google_Art_Project.jpg#mediaviewer/File:Edouard_Manet_-_Luncheon_on_the_Grass_-_Google_Art_Project.jpg

"Edouard Manet - Olympia - Google Art Project 3" by Édouard Manet - Google Art Project: Home - pic Maximum resolution. Colours edited by uploader. Licensed under Public domain via Wikimedia Commons - http://commons.wikimedia.org/wiki/File:Edouard_Manet_-_Olympia_-_Google_Art_Project_3.jpg#mediaviewer/File:Edouard_Manet_-_Olympia_-_Google_Art_Project_3.jpg

Olympia (Manet). (2014, September 7). In *Wikipedia, The Free Encyclopedia*. Retrieved 16:19, September 21, 2014, from http://en.wikipedia.org/w/index.php?title=Olympia_(Manet)&oldid=624524020

http://www.pbs.org/wgbh/cultureshock/beyond/manet.html

http://books.google.com/books?id=RdzCFocRauUC&pg=PA43&lpg=PA43&dq=%E2%80%9CWhat+is+this+Odalisque+with+a+yellow+stomach,+a+base+model+picked+up+I+know+not+where,+who+represents+Olympia?%E2%80%9D+%E2%80%93L%E2%80%99Artiste&source=bl&ots=X17rtcWS6-&sig=Ar5Ed1J8ztU76AV46k4toAsVz3E&hl=en&sa=X&ei=hC8bVNrfL4PYoATBrYKwCA&ved=0CCAQ6AEwAA#v=onepage&q=%E2%80%9CWhat%20is%20this%20Odalisque%20with%20a%20yellow%20stomach%2C%20a%20base%20model%20picked%20up%20I%20know%20not%20where%2C%20who%20represents%20Olympia%3F%E2%80%9D%20%E2%80%93L%E2%80%99Artiste&f=false

Henri Matisse. (2014, September 21). In *Wikipedia, The Free Encyclopedia*. Retrieved 16:19, September 21, 2014, from http://en.wikipedia.org/w/index.php?title=Henri_Matisse&oldid=626441271

http://www.newspapers.com/newspage/20419305/

"Matisse - Green Line". Via Wikipedia - http://en.wikipedia.org/wiki/File:Matisse_-_Green_Line.jpeg#mediaviewer/File:Matisse_-_Green_Line.jpeg

Claude Monet. (2014, September 15). In *Wikipedia, The Free Encyclopedia*. Retrieved 16:21, September 21, 2014, from
http://en.wikipedia.org/w/index.php?title=Claude_Monet&oldid=625719878

http://www.biography.com/people/claude-monet-9411771

https://flowboard.com/s/1709/C7B520B7-D289-4DCB-B587-02F182700802

http://jesscy.com/tag/claude-monet/

Le Bassin Aux Nymphéas. (2013, December 31). In *Wikipedia, The Free Encyclopedia*. Retrieved 16:22, September 21, 2014, from
http://en.wikipedia.org/w/index.php?title=Le_Bassin_Aux_Nymph%C3%A9as&oldid=588559047

"Le bassin aux nymphéas - Claude Monet" by Claude Monet - 1. Private collection2. Christie's, LotFinder: entry 5100003 (sale 7599, lot 16, london, 24 June 2008). Licensed under Public domain via Wikimedia Commons - http://commons.wikimedia.org/wiki/File:Le_bassin_aux_nymph%C3%A9as_-_Claude_Monet.jpg#mediaviewer/File:Le_bassin_aux_nymph%C3%A9as_-_Claude_Monet.jpg

Pablo Picasso. (2014, September 7). In *Wikipedia, The Free Encyclopedia*. Retrieved 03:15, September 19, 2014, from
http://en.wikipedia.org/w/index.php?title=Pablo_Picasso&oldid=624554925

Les Demoiselles d'Avignon. (2014, September 15). In *Wikipedia, The Free Encyclopedia*. Retrieved 16:38, September 21, 2014, from
http://en.wikipedia.org/w/index.php?title=Les_Demoiselles_d%27Avignon&oldid=625638888

"Les Demoiselles d'Avignon". Via Wikipedia -
http://en.wikipedia.org/wiki/File:Les_Demoiselles_d%27Avignon.jpg#mediaviewer/File:Les_Demoiselles_d%27Avignon.jpg

Pierre-Auguste Renoir. (2014, September 15). In *Wikipedia, The Free Encyclopedia*. Retrieved 03:20, September 19, 2014, from
http://en.wikipedia.org/w/index.php?title=Pierre-Auguste_Renoir&oldid=625708843

"Pierre-Auguste Renoir - Luncheon of the Boating Party - Google Art Project" by Pierre-Auguste Renoir - mgHsTKDNJVzPAg at Google Cultural Institute, zoom level maximum.

Licensed under Public domain via Wikimedia Commons - http://commons.wikimedia.org/wiki/File:Pierre-Auguste_Renoir_-_Luncheon_of_the_Boating_Party_-_Google_Art_Project.jpg#mediaviewer/File:Pierre-Auguste_Renoir_-_Luncheon_of_the_Boating_Party_-_Google_Art_Project.jpg

Auguste Rodin. (2014, September 3). In *Wikipedia, The Free Encyclopedia*. Retrieved 03:21, September 19, 2014, from http://en.wikipedia.org/w/index.php?title=Auguste_Rodin&oldid=623942523

http://www.musee-rodin.fr/en/auguste-rodin

The Thinker. (2014, May 9). In *Wikipedia, The Free Encyclopedia*. Retrieved 16:42, September 21, 2014, from http://en.wikipedia.org/w/index.php?title=The_Thinker&oldid=607709028

"Paris 2010 - Le Penseur" by Daniel Stockman - Flickr: Paris 2010 Day 3 - 9. Licensed under Creative Commons Attribution-Share Alike 2.0 via Wikimedia Commons - http://commons.wikimedia.org/wiki/File:Paris_2010_-_Le_Penseur.jpg#mediaviewer/File:Paris_2010_-_Le_Penseur.jpg

Henri de Toulouse-Lautrec. (2014, September 6). In *Wikipedia, The Free Encyclopedia*. Retrieved 02:49, September 20, 2014, from http://en.wikipedia.org/w/index.php?title=Henri_de_Toulouse-Lautrec&oldid=624391894

"Henri de Toulouse-Lautrec 018" by Henri de Toulouse-Lautrec - Matthias, Arnold: Henri de Toulouse-Lauterc, Taschen 1987, s. 17. Licensed under Public domain via Wikimedia Commons - http://commons.wikimedia.org/wiki/File:Henri_de_Toulouse-Lautrec_018.jpg#mediaviewer/File:Henri_de_Toulouse-Lautrec_018.jpg

Vincent van Gogh. (2014, September 10). In *Wikipedia, The Free Encyclopedia*. Retrieved 02:53, September 20, 2014, from http://en.wikipedia.org/w/index.php?title=Vincent_van_Gogh&oldid=624890096

"Vincent Willem van Gogh 102" by Vincent van Gogh - The Yorck Project: 10.000 Meisterwerke der Malerei. DVD-ROM, 2002. ISBN 3936122202. Distributed by DIRECTMEDIA Publishing GmbH.. Licensed under Public domain via Wikimedia Commons - http://commons.wikimedia.org/wiki/File:Vincent_Willem_van_Gogh_102.jpg#mediaviewer/File:Vincent_Willem_van_Gogh_102.jpg

Johannes Vermeer. (2014, September 3). In *Wikipedia, The Free Encyclopedia*. Retrieved 02:55, September 20, 2014, from http://en.wikipedia.org/w/index.php?title=Johannes_Vermeer&oldid=623965634

"Johannes Vermeer - Het melkmeisje - Google Art Project" by Johannes Vermeer - 9AHrwZ3Av6Zhjg at Google Cultural Institute, zoom level maximum. Licensed under Public domain via Wikimedia Commons - http://commons.wikimedia.org/wiki/File:Johannes_Vermeer_-_Het_melkmeisje_-_Google_Art_Project.jpg#mediaviewer/File:Johannes_Vermeer_-_Het_melkmeisje_-_Google_Art_Project.jpg

Chester Carlson. (2014, September 12). In *Wikipedia, The Free Encyclopedia*. Retrieved 02:58, September 20, 2014, from
http://en.wikipedia.org/w/index.php?title=Chester_Carlson&oldid=625282431

Mark Cuban. (2014, September 15). In *Wikipedia, The Free Encyclopedia*. Retrieved 03:01, September 20, 2014, from
http://en.wikipedia.org/w/index.php?title=Mark_Cuban&oldid=625715571

http://getbusylivingblog.com/famous-people-who-found-success-despite-failures/

Walt Disney. (2014, September 11). In *Wikipedia, The Free Encyclopedia*. Retrieved 03:02, September 20, 2014, from
http://en.wikipedia.org/w/index.php?title=Walt_Disney&oldid=625016407

http://www.hollywoodstories.com/pages/disney/d3.html

http://www.businessinsider.com/15-people-who-were-fired-before-they-became-filthy-rich-2011-4?op=1

http://thewaltdisneycompany.com/investors/financial-information/annual-report

Henry Ford. (2014, September 11). In *Wikipedia, The Free Encyclopedia*. Retrieved 03:04, September 20, 2014, from
http://en.wikipedia.org/w/index.php?title=Henry_Ford&oldid=625165489

Chris Gardner. (2014, August 13). In *Wikipedia, The Free Encyclopedia*. Retrieved 03:05, September 20, 2014, from
http://en.wikipedia.org/w/index.php?title=Chris_Gardner&oldid=621129839

Bill Gates. (2014, September 6). *Wikiquote,* . Retrieved 03:06, September 20, 2014 from http://en.wikiquote.org/w/index.php?title=Bill_Gates&oldid=1781684.

Bill Gates. (2014, September 18). In *Wikipedia, The Free Encyclopedia*. Retrieved 03:07, September 20, 2014, from
http://en.wikipedia.org/w/index.php?title=Bill_Gates&oldid=626023764

Soichiro Honda. (2014, August 25). In *Wikipedia, The Free Encyclopedia*. Retrieved 03:08, September 20, 2014, from
http://en.wikipedia.org/w/index.php?title=Soichiro_Honda&oldid=622782936

Steve Jobs. (2014, September 17). In *Wikipedia, The Free Encyclopedia*. Retrieved 03:09, September 20, 2014, from http://en.wikipedia.org/w/index.php?title=Steve_Jobs&oldid=625979527

http://news.stanford.edu/news/2005/june15/jobs-061505.html

http://www.cbsnews.com/news/alibaba-chairman-jack-ma-brings-company-to-america/

Rowland Hussey Macy. (2014, September 19). In *Wikipedia, The Free Encyclopedia*. Retrieved 03:10, September 20, 2014, from http://en.wikipedia.org/w/index.php?title=Rowland_Hussey_Macy&oldid=626252432

Akio Morita. (2014, September 16). In *Wikipedia, The Free Encyclopedia*. Retrieved 03:11, September 20, 2014, from http://en.wikipedia.org/w/index.php?title=Akio_Morita&oldid=625787034

Sumner Redstone. (2014, August 9). In *Wikipedia, The Free Encyclopedia*. Retrieved 03:13, September 20, 2014, from http://en.wikipedia.org/w/index.php?title=Sumner_Redstone&oldid=620561134

http://www.brainyquote.com/quotes/quotes/s/sumnerreds227812.html

Colonel Sanders. (2014, September 8). In *Wikipedia, The Free Encyclopedia*. Retrieved 03:14, September 20, 2014, from http://en.wikipedia.org/w/index.php?title=Colonel_Sanders&oldid=624700542

http://colonelsanders.com/bio.asp

http://www.cnn.com/2013/01/21/us/steven-spielberg-fast-facts/

http://www.theblackandblue.com/2011/04/05/the-steven-spielberg-three-step-guide-to-rejection/

Steven Spielberg. (2014, September 19). In *Wikipedia, The Free Encyclopedia*. Retrieved 03:18, September 20, 2014, from http://en.wikipedia.org/w/index.php?title=Steven_Spielberg&oldid=626185886

Ted Turner. (2014, September 13). In *Wikipedia, The Free Encyclopedia*. Retrieved 03:19, September 20, 2014, from http://en.wikipedia.org/w/index.php?title=Ted_Turner&oldid=625447271

http://www.newser.com/story/84148/9-successes-who-were-rejected-by-colleges.html

Oprah Winfrey. (2014, September 9). In *Wikipedia, The Free Encyclopedia*. Retrieved 03:21, September 20, 2014, from http://en.wikipedia.org/w/index.php?title=Oprah_Winfrey&oldid=624750041

F. W. Woolworth Company. (2014, September 8). In *Wikipedia, The Free Encyclopedia*. Retrieved 03:22, September 20, 2014, from http://en.wikipedia.org/w/index.php?title=F._W._Woolworth_Company&oldid=624712090

http://blogs.baruch.cuny.edu/overcomingadversity/stories/businesspeople/

Nick Woodman. (2014, September 15). In *Wikipedia, The Free Encyclopedia*. Retrieved 03:24, September 20, 2014, from http://en.wikipedia.org/w/index.php?title=Nick_Woodman&oldid=625644901

GoPro. (2014, September 19). In *Wikipedia, The Free Encyclopedia*. Retrieved 03:24, September 20, 2014, from http://en.wikipedia.org/w/index.php?title=GoPro&oldid=626254479

http://jewishbusinessnews.com/2013/03/07/welcome-to-the-billionaires-club/

http://www.achievement.org/autodoc/page/smi0pro-1

Academy Award for Best Picture. (2014, September 17). In *Wikipedia, The Free Encyclopedia*. Retrieved 03:55, September 20, 2014, from http://en.wikipedia.org/w/index.php?title=Academy_Award_for_Best_Picture&oldid=625883191

http://www.afi.com/100years/movies10.aspx

http://www.ajc.com/

http://www.theatlantic.com/

http://www.baltimoresun.com/

http://www.tvweek.com/open-mic/2012/11/the-most-outrageous-experiment-even-conducted-in-the-movie-industry-do-those-working-in-the-movies-k/

http://www.chicagoreader.com/

http://www.suntimes.com/

http://www.chicagotribune.com/

http://www.csmonitor.com/

http://www.deseretnews.com/home/

http://www.ew.com/ew/

http://www.filmthreat.com/

Pauline Kael. (2014, September 3). In *Wikipedia, The Free Encyclopedia*. Retrieved 04:05, September 20, 2014, from http://en.wikipedia.org/w/index.php?title=Pauline_Kael&oldid=624059598

http://www.slate.com/blogs/browbeat/2011/10/28/pauline_kael_reviews_the_ones_she_got_wrong.html

http://www.latimes.com/

http://www.metacritic.com/

http://www.newrepublic.com/

http://www.newsday.com/

http://observer.com/

http://nypress.com/

http://www.newstatesman.com/

http://www.newyorker.com/books/double-take/five-classic-pauline-kael-reviews

http://nymag.com/

http://www.nydailynews.com/

http://www.nytimes.com/

http://www.people.com/people/

http://www.philly.com/

http://www.rogerebert.com/

http://www.rottentomatoes.com/

http://www.sfexaminer.com/

http://time.com/

http://www.timeout.com/london

http://www.thestar.com/

http://variety.com/

http://www.villagevoice.com/

http://www.washingtonpost.com/

http://www.denofgeek.us/movies/22058/the-hit-films-hollywood-studios-didn-t-want

Winston Churchill. (2014, September 15). In *Wikipedia, The Free Encyclopedia*. Retrieved 04:10, September 20, 2014, from
http://en.wikipedia.org/w/index.php?title=Winston_Churchill&oldid=625643894

http://www.lehrmaninstitute.org/education/the-education-of-winston-churchill%20.html

Charles Darwin. (2014, September 7). In *Wikipedia, The Free Encyclopedia*. Retrieved 04:11, September 20, 2014, from
http://en.wikipedia.org/w/index.php?title=Charles_Darwin&oldid=624556932

Albert Einstein. (2014, September 15). In *Wikipedia, The Free Encyclopedia*. Retrieved 04:13, September 20, 2014, from
http://en.wikipedia.org/w/index.php?title=Albert_Einstein&oldid=625676834

http://www.brainyquote.com/quotes/authors/a/albert_einstein.html

Dwight D. Eisenhower. (2014, September 19). In *Wikipedia, The Free Encyclopedia*. Retrieved 04:15, September 20, 2014, from
http://en.wikipedia.org/w/index.php?title=Dwight_D._Eisenhower&oldid=626223989

Robert H. Goddard. (2014, September 14). In *Wikipedia, The Free Encyclopedia*. Retrieved 04:15, September 20, 2014, from
http://en.wikipedia.org/w/index.php?title=Robert_H._Goddard&oldid=625554801

Ulysses S. Grant. (2014, September 8). In *Wikipedia, The Free Encyclopedia*. Retrieved 04:16, September 20, 2014, from
http://en.wikipedia.org/w/index.php?title=Ulysses_S._Grant&oldid=624614039

Martin Luther King, Jr.. (2014, September 17). In *Wikipedia, The Free Encyclopedia*. Retrieved 04:17, September 20, 2014, from
http://en.wikipedia.org/w/index.php?title=Martin_Luther_King,_Jr.&oldid=625998776

Abraham Lincoln. (2014, September 19). In *Wikipedia, The Free Encyclopedia*. Retrieved 04:18, September 20, 2014, from
http://en.wikipedia.org/w/index.php?title=Abraham_Lincoln&oldid=626249177

http://www.theatlantic.com/magazine/archive/2005/10/lincolns-great-depression/304247/

Nelson Mandela. (2014, September 15). In *Wikipedia, The Free Encyclopedia*. Retrieved 04:19, September 20, 2014, from
http://en.wikipedia.org/w/index.php?title=Nelson_Mandela&oldid=625615628

John D. Rockefeller. (2014, September 16). In *Wikipedia, The Free Encyclopedia*. Retrieved 04:20, September 20, 2014, from
http://en.wikipedia.org/w/index.php?title=John_D._Rockefeller&oldid=625829703

Theodore Roosevelt. (2014, September 19). In *Wikipedia, The Free Encyclopedia*. Retrieved 04:20, September 20, 2014, from
http://en.wikipedia.org/w/index.php?title=Theodore_Roosevelt&oldid=626215388

http://www.nps.gov/history/history/hisnps/npshistory/teddy.htm

Socrates. (2014, September 13). In *Wikipedia, The Free Encyclopedia*. Retrieved 04:23, September 20, 2014, from
http://en.wikipedia.org/w/index.php?title=Socrates&oldid=625442467

Wright brothers. (2014, September 17). In *Wikipedia, The Free Encyclopedia*. Retrieved 04:24, September 20, 2014, from
http://en.wikipedia.org/w/index.php?title=Wright_brothers&oldid=625999180

http://www.spaciousplanet.com/world/new/the-50-worst-predictions-of-all-time

http://www.who.int/bulletin/volumes/86/8/08-056242/en/

http://www.msthalloffame.org/spencer_silver.htm

http://articles.latimes.com/1999/dec/31/local/me-49395

http://inventors.about.com/od/famousinventions/tp/bad-predictions.htm

The Beatles. (2014, September 19). In *Wikipedia, The Free Encyclopedia*. Retrieved 05:30, September 20, 2014, from
http://en.wikipedia.org/w/index.php?title=The_Beatles&oldid=626175764

The Beatles' Decca audition. (2014, June 23). In *Wikipedia, The Free Encyclopedia*. Retrieved 05:32, September 20, 2014, from

http://en.wikipedia.org/w/index.php?title=The_Beatles%27_Decca_audition&oldid=614028295

http://articles.latimes.com/2014/feb/09/opinion/la-oe-beatles-quotes-20140209

Ludwig van Beethoven. (2014, September 13). In *Wikipedia, The Free Encyclopedia*. Retrieved 05:34, September 20, 2014, from http://en.wikipedia.org/w/index.php?title=Ludwig_van_Beethoven&oldid=625402621

Georges Bizet. (2014, September 4). In *Wikipedia, The Free Encyclopedia*. Retrieved 05:35, September 20, 2014, from http://en.wikipedia.org/w/index.php?title=Georges_Bizet&oldid=624119227

http://www.bostonglobe.com/

Enrico Caruso. (2014, September 2). In *Wikipedia, The Free Encyclopedia*. Retrieved 05:38, September 20, 2014, from http://en.wikipedia.org/w/index.php?title=Enrico_Caruso&oldid=623827693

http://www.robertchristgau.com/

http://www.ew.com/ew/

http://www.theguardian.com/uk

http://www.independent.co.uk/

http://www.metacritic.com/music

http://www.lettersofnote.com/2011/01/i-do-not-feel-that-madonna-is-ready-yet.html

Wolfgang Amadeus Mozart. (2014, September 12). In *Wikipedia, The Free Encyclopedia*. Retrieved 05:47, September 20, 2014, from http://en.wikipedia.org/w/index.php?title=Wolfgang_Amadeus_Mozart&oldid=625220969

http://www.nme.com/

Katy Perry. (2014, November 26). In *Wikipedia, The Free Encyclopedia*. Retrieved 22:24, November 26, 2014, from http://en.wikipedia.org/w/index.php?title=Katy_Perry&oldid=635540340

Elvis Presley. (2014, September 13). In *Wikipedia, The Free Encyclopedia*. Retrieved 05:52, September 20, 2014, from http://en.wikipedia.org/w/index.php?title=Elvis_Presley&oldid=625447434

http://rateyourmusic.com/list/schmidtt/rolling_stones_500_worst_reviews_of_all_time_work_in_progress_/

http://www.rollingstone.com/

Igor Stravinsky. (2014, September 16). In *Wikipedia, The Free Encyclopedia*. Retrieved 05:54, September 20, 2014, from http://en.wikipedia.org/w/index.php?title=Igor_Stravinsky&oldid=625879614

The Rite of Spring. (2014, September 2). In *Wikipedia, The Free Encyclopedia*. Retrieved 05:55, September 20, 2014, from http://en.wikipedia.org/w/index.php?title=The_Rite_of_Spring&oldid=623835538

http://loudwire.com/record-company-vulgar-rejection-letter-venom-unveiled/

http://www.nytimes.com/2008/03/30/books/review/Brockes-t.html?pagewanted=print&_r=0

Julie Andrews. (2014, September 3). In *Wikipedia, The Free Encyclopedia*. Retrieved 05:57, September 20, 2014, from http://en.wikipedia.org/w/index.php?title=Julie_Andrews&oldid=623945130

Fred Astaire. (2014, September 18). In *Wikipedia, The Free Encyclopedia*. Retrieved 16:32, September 20, 2014, from http://en.wikipedia.org/w/index.php?title=Fred_Astaire&oldid=626077887

http://www.biography.com/people/fred-astaire-9190991

Fred Astaire. (2014, September 11). *Wikiquote,* . Retrieved 16:36, September 20, 2014 from http://en.wikiquote.org/w/index.php?title=Fred_Astaire&oldid=1784069.

http://quoteinvestigator.com/2014/08/07/bald/

Lucille Ball. (2014, September 11). In *Wikipedia, The Free Encyclopedia*. Retrieved 16:40, September 20, 2014, from http://en.wikipedia.org/w/index.php?title=Lucille_Ball&oldid=625162005

http://www.biography.com/people/lucille-ball-9196958

Michael Caine. (2014, September 17). In *Wikipedia, The Free Encyclopedia*. Retrieved 16:43, September 20, 2014, from http://en.wikipedia.org/w/index.php?title=Michael_Caine&oldid=625949065

Charlie Chaplin. (2014, September 20). In *Wikipedia, The Free Encyclopedia*. Retrieved 16:43, September 20, 2014, from http://en.wikipedia.org/w/index.php?title=Charlie_Chaplin&oldid=626277657

Harrison Ford. (2014, September 19). In *Wikipedia, The Free Encyclopedia*. Retrieved 16:46, September 20, 2014, from
http://en.wikipedia.org/w/index.php?title=Harrison_Ford&oldid=626190141

http://teamcoco.com/video/harrison-ford-was-told-he-d-never-be-a-star

Phil Hartman. (2014, September 19). In *Wikipedia, The Free Encyclopedia*. Retrieved 17:08, September 20, 2014, from
http://en.wikipedia.org/w/index.php?title=Phil_Hartman&oldid=626270082

Harvey Keitel. (2014, September 12). In *Wikipedia, The Free Encyclopedia*. Retrieved 17:09, September 20, 2014, from
http://en.wikipedia.org/w/index.php?title=Harvey_Keitel&oldid=625302642

https://www.youtube.com/watch?v=8UYI6L974KY

http://books.google.com/books?id=q1YjSR6VOKEC&pg=PA196&lpg=PA196&dq=emmeline+snively+marilyn+monroe+be+a+secretary+instead&source=bl&ots=j5SQmZnIP5&sig=OLcYm1IqRCqI5hjkhvm9iXc5mfg&hl=en&sa=X&ei=dz8JVKXMNKiBiwK7zYGQCw&ved=0CCYQ6AEwAQ#v=onepage&q=emmeline%20snively%20marilyn%20monroe%20be%20a%20secretary%20instead&f=false

Marilyn Monroe. (2014, September 19). In *Wikipedia, The Free Encyclopedia*. Retrieved 17:11, September 20, 2014, from
http://en.wikipedia.org/w/index.php?title=Marilyn_Monroe&oldid=626258361

Jeanne Moreau. (2014, September 14). In *Wikipedia, The Free Encyclopedia*. Retrieved 17:12, September 20, 2014, from
http://en.wikipedia.org/w/index.php?title=Jeanne_Moreau&oldid=625559814

http://www.imdb.com/name/nm0603402/

http://www.businessinsider.com/15-people-who-failed-before-becoming-famous-2012-10?op=1

Sidney Poitier. (2014, August 10). In *Wikipedia, The Free Encyclopedia*. Retrieved 17:14, September 20, 2014, from
http://en.wikipedia.org/w/index.php?title=Sidney_Poitier&oldid=620679530

Jerry Seinfeld. (2014, September 18). In *Wikipedia, The Free Encyclopedia*. Retrieved 17:15, September 20, 2014, from
http://en.wikipedia.org/w/index.php?title=Jerry_Seinfeld&oldid=626018807

Sylvester Stallone. (2014, September 20). In *Wikipedia, The Free Encyclopedia*. Retrieved 17:19, September 20, 2014, from http://en.wikipedia.org/w/index.php?title=Sylvester_Stallone&oldid=626337798

http://www.nytimes.com/packages/html/movies/bestpictures/rocky-ar.html

http://totalrocky.com/articles/sylvester-stallone-rocky-road-to-riches.html

Rocky. (2014, September 19). In *Wikipedia, The Free Encyclopedia*. Retrieved 17:23, September 20, 2014, from http://en.wikipedia.org/w/index.php?title=Rocky&oldid=626185093

http://www.news.com.au/entertainment/movies/sylvester-stallone-sells-dog-for-50-then-buys-it-back-for-3k/story-e6frfmvr-1226566450993

Glenn Cunningham (athlete). (2014, July 14). In *Wikipedia, The Free Encyclopedia*. Retrieved 17:27, September 20, 2014, from http://en.wikipedia.org/w/index.php?title=Glenn_Cunningham_(athlete)&oldid=616934418

Jack Johnson (boxer). (2014, September 16). In *Wikipedia, The Free Encyclopedia*. Retrieved 17:28, September 20, 2014, from http://en.wikipedia.org/w/index.php?title=Jack_Johnson_(boxer)&oldid=625841693

Michael Jordan. (2014, September 4). In *Wikipedia, The Free Encyclopedia*. Retrieved 17:29, September 20, 2014, from http://en.wikipedia.org/w/index.php?title=Michael_Jordan&oldid=624118238

http://www.nytimes.com/2012/02/25/sports/basketball/lins-new-challenge-media-onslaught-at-all-star-weekend.html?_r=0

Jeremy Lin. (2014, September 3). In *Wikipedia, The Free Encyclopedia*. Retrieved 17:30, September 20, 2014, from http://en.wikipedia.org/w/index.php?title=Jeremy_Lin&oldid=624053985

Manny Pacquiao. (2014, September 12). In *Wikipedia, The Free Encyclopedia*. Retrieved 17:31, September 20, 2014, from http://en.wikipedia.org/w/index.php?title=Manny_Pacquiao&oldid=625206189

Wilma Rudolph. (2014, September 6). In *Wikipedia, The Free Encyclopedia*. Retrieved 17:31, September 20, 2014, from http://en.wikipedia.org/w/index.php?title=Wilma_Rudolph&oldid=624379282

Babe Ruth. (2014, September 2). In *Wikipedia, The Free Encyclopedia*. Retrieved 17:32, September 20, 2014, from http://en.wikipedia.org/w/index.php?title=Babe_Ruth&oldid=623926221

Jim Thorpe. (2014, September 7). In *Wikipedia, The Free Encyclopedia*. Retrieved 17:33, September 20, 2014, from http://en.wikipedia.org/w/index.php?title=Jim_Thorpe&oldid=624509206

Johnny Unitas. (2014, September 14). In *Wikipedia, The Free Encyclopedia*. Retrieved 17:33, September 20, 2014, from http://en.wikipedia.org/w/index.php?title=Johnny_Unitas&oldid=625516368

http://www.bostonglobe.com/

http://www.suntimes.com/

http://www.hollywoodreporter.com/

http://www.metacritic.com/tv

http://www.miamiherald.com/

http://www.newrepublic.com/

http://www.nydailynews.com/

http://www.newyorker.com/

http://nypost.com/

http://www.nytimes.com/

http://www.newsday.com/

http://www.orlandosentinel.com/

http://www.philly.com/

http://www.utsandiego.com/

http://time.com/

http://www.usatoday.com/

http://online.wsj.com/home-page

http://www.washingtonpost.com/

https://www.youtube.com/watch?v=t9mtPhZEJoQ

http://magazine.foxnews.com/celebrity/10-things-you-didnt-know-about-breaking-bad

http://www.minyanville.com/special-features/articles/cosby-abc-nbc-ge-disney-viacom/4/23/2010/id/27121

http://www.neatorama.com/2008/04/15/the-stupidest-business-decisions-in-history/

http://www.tvguide.com/News/Seinfeld-Research-Memo-1083639.aspx

http://deadline.com/2013/01/deja-vu-13-years-after-csi-abc-studios-pulls-out-of-another-anthony-zuiker-project-416434/

http://www.gq.com/entertainment/movies-and-tv/201206/roundtable-discussion-matthew-weiner-vince-gilligan-david-milch?currentPage=1

http://www.today.com/entertainment/christina-hendricks-agency-dropped-me-doing-mad-men-1D80012811?utm_source=zergnet.com&utm_medium=referral&utm_campaign=zergnet_235000

http://www.azevedosreviews.com/2013/05/28/bukowskis-10-quotes-on-writing/

http://www.onehundredrejections.com/2012/06/famous-rejection-76-chinua-achebes.html

Chinua Achebe. (2014, September 12). In *Wikipedia, The Free Encyclopedia*. Retrieved 17:59, September 20, 2014, from http://en.wikipedia.org/w/index.php?title=Chinua_Achebe&oldid=625302080

http://www.litlovers.com/reading-guides/13-fiction/1036-things-fall-apart-achebe?start=1

Watership Down. (2014, September 19). In *Wikipedia, The Free Encyclopedia*. Retrieved 18:01, September 20, 2014, from http://en.wikipedia.org/w/index.php?title=Watership_Down&oldid=626158795

Louisa May Alcott. (2014, September 11). In *Wikipedia, The Free Encyclopedia*. Retrieved 18:06, September 20, 2014, from http://en.wikipedia.org/w/index.php?title=Louisa_May_Alcott&oldid=625110866

https://historysmiths.com/Alcott.html

Winesburg, Ohio (novel). (2014, February 25). In *Wikipedia, The Free Encyclopedia*. Retrieved 18:43, September 20, 2014, from http://en.wikipedia.org/w/index.php?title=Winesburg,_Ohio_(novel)&oldid=596997691

Richard Bach. (2014, August 4). In *Wikipedia, The Free Encyclopedia*. Retrieved 18:50, September 20, 2014, from http://en.wikipedia.org/w/index.php?title=Richard_Bach&oldid=619768655

Jonathan Livingston Seagull. (2014, September 15). In *Wikipedia, The Free Encyclopedia*. Retrieved 18:51, September 20, 2014, from http://en.wikipedia.org/w/index.php?title=Jonathan_Livingston_Seagull&oldid=625687343

http://www.rogerebert.com/reviews/jonathan-livingston-seagull-1973

http://www.literaryrejections.com/best-sellers-initially-rejected/

The Wonderful Wizard of Oz. (2014, September 12). In *Wikipedia, The Free Encyclopedia*. Retrieved 18:53, September 20, 2014, from http://en.wikipedia.org/w/index.php?title=The_Wonderful_Wizard_of_Oz&oldid=625228912

Crash (J. G. Ballard novel). (2014, August 4). In *Wikipedia, The Free Encyclopedia*. Retrieved 18:54, September 20, 2014, from http://en.wikipedia.org/w/index.php?title=Crash_(J._G._Ballard_novel)&oldid=619756960

http://www.newyorker.com/books/page-turner/j-g-ballard

James Baldwin. (2014, September 18). In *Wikipedia, The Free Encyclopedia*. Retrieved 18:56, September 20, 2014, from http://en.wikipedia.org/w/index.php?title=James_Baldwin&oldid=626046271

http://www.literaryrejections.com/best-sellers-initially-rejected/

Judy Blume. (2014, September 13). In *Wikipedia, The Free Encyclopedia*. Retrieved 18:57, September 20, 2014, from http://en.wikipedia.org/w/index.php?title=Judy_Blume&oldid=625399899

http://judyblume.com/writing/rejection.php

Jorge Luis Borges. (2014, September 19). In *Wikipedia, The Free Encyclopedia*. Retrieved 18:59, September 20, 2014, from http://en.wikipedia.org/w/index.php?title=Jorge_Luis_Borges&oldid=626261997

Wuthering Heights. (2014, September 18). In *Wikipedia, The Free Encyclopedia*. Retrieved 19:00, September 20, 2014, from http://en.wikipedia.org/w/index.php?title=Wuthering_Heights&oldid=626027765

The Da Vinci Code. (2014, September 16). In *Wikipedia, The Free Encyclopedia*. Retrieved 19:01, September 20, 2014, from http://en.wikipedia.org/w/index.php?title=The_Da_Vinci_Code&oldid=625757405

Dan Brown. (2014, September 18). In *Wikipedia, The Free Encyclopedia*. Retrieved 19:02, September 20, 2014, from http://en.wikipedia.org/w/index.php?title=Dan_Brown&oldid=626134213

Pearl S. Buck. (2014, September 6). In *Wikipedia, The Free Encyclopedia*. Retrieved 19:03, September 20, 2014, from http://en.wikipedia.org/w/index.php?title=Pearl_S._Buck&oldid=624413317

Tarzan. (2014, September 14). In *Wikipedia, The Free Encyclopedia*. Retrieved 19:04, September 20, 2014, from http://en.wikipedia.org/w/index.php?title=Tarzan&oldid=625464069

Edgar Rice Burroughs. (2014, July 28). In *Wikipedia, The Free Encyclopedia*. Retrieved 19:05, September 20, 2014, from http://en.wikipedia.org/w/index.php?title=Edgar_Rice_Burroughs&oldid=618856306

http://dearauthor.com/features/interviews/my-first-sale-by-meg-cabot/

The Princess Diaries. (2014, September 7). In *Wikipedia, The Free Encyclopedia*. Retrieved 19:06, September 20, 2014, from http://en.wikipedia.org/w/index.php?title=The_Princess_Diaries&oldid=624514963

http://www.chickensoup.com/about/history

Chicken Soup for the Soul. (2014, September 11). In *Wikipedia, The Free Encyclopedia*. Retrieved 19:32, September 20, 2014, from http://en.wikipedia.org/w/index.php?title=Chicken_Soup_for_the_Soul&oldid=625069291

Agatha Christie. (2014, September 17). In *Wikipedia, The Free Encyclopedia*. Retrieved 19:33, September 20, 2014, from http://en.wikipedia.org/w/index.php?title=Agatha_Christie&oldid=626004017

http://www.forbes.com/sites/kiriblakeley/2011/04/04/at-83-mary-higgins-clark-is-still-a-publishing-powerhouse/

Mary Higgins Clark. (2014, September 3). In *Wikipedia, The Free Encyclopedia*. Retrieved 19:35, September 20, 2014, from http://en.wikipedia.org/w/index.php?title=Mary_Higgins_Clark&oldid=623993078

The Alchemist (novel). (2014, September 12). In *Wikipedia, The Free Encyclopedia*. Retrieved 19:37, September 20, 2014, from http://en.wikipedia.org/w/index.php?title=The_Alchemist_(novel)&oldid=625280105

E. E. Cummings. (2014, September 20). In *Wikipedia, The Free Encyclopedia*. Retrieved 19:38, September 20, 2014, from http://en.wikipedia.org/w/index.php?title=E._E._Cummings&oldid=626376382

http://mentalfloss.com/article/49171/7-book-dedications-basically-say-screw-you

Patrick Dennis. (2014, March 23). In *Wikipedia, The Free Encyclopedia*. Retrieved 19:41, September 20, 2014, from http://en.wikipedia.org/w/index.php?title=Patrick_Dennis&oldid=600832839

Emily Dickinson. (2014, September 6). In *Wikipedia, The Free Encyclopedia*. Retrieved 19:42, September 20, 2014, from http://en.wikipedia.org/w/index.php?title=Emily_Dickinson&oldid=624403517

William Faulkner. (2014, September 16). In *Wikipedia, The Free Encyclopedia*. Retrieved 19:44, September 20, 2014, from http://en.wikipedia.org/w/index.php?title=William_Faulkner&oldid=625802847

http://www.nytimes.com/books/00/12/24/specials/fitzgerald-gatsby60.html

The Great Gatsby. (2014, September 19). In *Wikipedia, The Free Encyclopedia*. Retrieved 19:46, September 20, 2014, from http://en.wikipedia.org/w/index.php?title=The_Great_Gatsby&oldid=626219183

F. Scott Fitzgerald. (2014, September 18). In *Wikipedia, The Free Encyclopedia*. Retrieved 19:47, September 20, 2014, from http://en.wikipedia.org/w/index.php?title=F._Scott_Fitzgerald&oldid=626046173

The Eyre Affair. (2014, April 23). In *Wikipedia, The Free Encyclopedia*. Retrieved 19:50, September 20, 2014, from http://en.wikipedia.org/w/index.php?title=The_Eyre_Affair&oldid=605471947

Madame Bovary. (2014, September 19). In *Wikipedia, The Free Encyclopedia*. Retrieved 19:54, September 20, 2014, from http://en.wikipedia.org/w/index.php?title=Madame_Bovary&oldid=626253553

Anne Frank. (2014, September 10). In *Wikipedia, The Free Encyclopedia*. Retrieved 19:58, September 20, 2014, from http://en.wikipedia.org/w/index.php?title=Anne_Frank&oldid=625002104

The Diary of a Young Girl. (2014, September 15). In *Wikipedia, The Free Encyclopedia*. Retrieved 20:00, September 20, 2014, from http://en.wikipedia.org/w/index.php?title=The_Diary_of_a_Young_Girl&oldid=625705322

Lord of the Flies. (2014, September 12). In *Wikipedia, The Free Encyclopedia*. Retrieved 20:01, September 20, 2014, from http://en.wikipedia.org/w/index.php?title=Lord_of_the_Flies&oldid=625209279

Kenneth Grahame. (2014, September 8). In *Wikipedia, The Free Encyclopedia*. Retrieved 20:08, September 20, 2014, from http://en.wikipedia.org/w/index.php?title=Kenneth_Grahame&oldid=624672870

The Wind in the Willows. (2014, September 18). In *Wikipedia, The Free Encyclopedia*. Retrieved 20:07, September 20, 2014, from http://en.wikipedia.org/w/index.php?title=The_Wind_in_the_Willows&oldid=626024331

Zane Grey. (2014, September 4). In *Wikipedia, The Free Encyclopedia*. Retrieved 20:09, September 20, 2014, from http://en.wikipedia.org/w/index.php?title=Zane_Grey&oldid=624193173

John Grisham. (2014, September 18). In *Wikipedia, The Free Encyclopedia*. Retrieved 20:10, September 20, 2014, from http://en.wikipedia.org/w/index.php?title=John_Grisham&oldid=626035678

A Time to Kill (Grisham novel). (2014, August 28). In *Wikipedia, The Free Encyclopedia*. Retrieved 20:11, September 20, 2014, from http://en.wikipedia.org/w/index.php?title=A_Time_to_Kill_(Grisham_novel)&oldid=623241908

Alex Haley. (2014, September 14). In *Wikipedia, The Free Encyclopedia*. Retrieved 20:12, September 20, 2014, from http://en.wikipedia.org/w/index.php?title=Alex_Haley&oldid=625589552

http://www.biography.com/people/alex-haley-39420

Roots: The Saga of an American Family. (2014, August 24). In *Wikipedia, The Free Encyclopedia*. Retrieved 20:13, September 20, 2014, from http://en.wikipedia.org/w/index.php?title=Roots:_The_Saga_of_an_American_Family&oldid=622608012

Catch-22. (2014, September 16). In *Wikipedia, The Free Encyclopedia*. Retrieved 20:15, September 20, 2014, from http://en.wikipedia.org/w/index.php?title=Catch-22&oldid=625754632

Ernest Hemingway. (2014, September 13). In *Wikipedia, The Free Encyclopedia*. Retrieved 20:18, September 20, 2014, from http://en.wikipedia.org/w/index.php?title=Ernest_Hemingway&oldid=625407708

http://www.nytimes.com/books/99/07/04/specials/hemingway-reviews.html

http://maisonneuve.org/article/2005/05/13/ernest-hemingways-lost-rejection-letter/

Frank Herbert. (2014, September 16). In *Wikipedia, The Free Encyclopedia*. Retrieved 20:23, September 20, 2014, from http://en.wikipedia.org/w/index.php?title=Frank_Herbert&oldid=625851423

Dune (novel). (2014, September 18). In *Wikipedia, The Free Encyclopedia*. Retrieved 20:20, September 20, 2014, from http://en.wikipedia.org/w/index.php?title=Dune_(novel)&oldid=626046355

Thor Heyerdahl. (2014, September 12). In *Wikipedia, The Free Encyclopedia*. Retrieved 20:24, September 20, 2014, from http://en.wikipedia.org/w/index.php?title=Thor_Heyerdahl&oldid=625229384

Kon-Tiki. (2014, September 12). In *Wikipedia, The Free Encyclopedia*. Retrieved 20:22, September 20, 2014, from http://en.wikipedia.org/w/index.php?title=Kon-Tiki&oldid=625229018

Tony Hillerman. (2014, September 14). In *Wikipedia, The Free Encyclopedia*. Retrieved 20:25, September 20, 2014, from http://en.wikipedia.org/w/index.php?title=Tony_Hillerman&oldid=625587529

The Kite Runner. (2014, September 20). In *Wikipedia, The Free Encyclopedia*. Retrieved 20:29, September 20, 2014, from http://en.wikipedia.org/w/index.php?title=The_Kite_Runner&oldid=626288893

James Joyce. (2014, September 14). In *Wikipedia, The Free Encyclopedia*. Retrieved 20:30, September 20, 2014, from http://en.wikipedia.org/w/index.php?title=James_Joyce&oldid=625539924

http://rmc.library.cornell.edu/joyce/earlyprose/

http://www.john-keats.com/biografie/blackwood.htm

John Keats. (2014, September 16). In *Wikipedia, The Free Encyclopedia*. Retrieved 20:32, September 20, 2014, from http://en.wikipedia.org/w/index.php?title=John_Keats&oldid=625811246

Ironweed (novel). (2014, September 10). In *Wikipedia, The Free Encyclopedia*. Retrieved 20:33, September 20, 2014, from
http://en.wikipedia.org/w/index.php?title=Ironweed_(novel)&oldid=624896372

Jack Kerouac. (2014, September 18). In *Wikipedia, The Free Encyclopedia*. Retrieved 20:35, September 20, 2014, from
http://en.wikipedia.org/w/index.php?title=Jack_Kerouac&oldid=626046261

On the Road. (2014, September 2). In *Wikipedia, The Free Encyclopedia*. Retrieved 20:36, September 20, 2014, from
http://en.wikipedia.org/w/index.php?title=On_the_Road&oldid=623849631

Daniel Keyes. (2014, September 9). In *Wikipedia, The Free Encyclopedia*. Retrieved 20:40, September 20, 2014, from
http://en.wikipedia.org/w/index.php?title=Daniel_Keyes&oldid=624788658

http://www.danielkeyesauthor.com/faq.html

Flowers for Algernon. (2014, September 17). In *Wikipedia, The Free Encyclopedia*. Retrieved 20:39, September 20, 2014, from
http://en.wikipedia.org/w/index.php?title=Flowers_for_Algernon&oldid=625896534

http://www.amazon.com/Think-Grow-Rich-Black-Choice/dp/0449219984

http://aalbc.com/reviews/so_you_wanna_write_a_best_seller.htm

Stephen King. (2014, September 20). In *Wikipedia, The Free Encyclopedia*. Retrieved 20:44, September 20, 2014, from
http://en.wikipedia.org/w/index.php?title=Stephen_King&oldid=626358089

Carrie (novel). (2014, September 14). In *Wikipedia, The Free Encyclopedia*. Retrieved 20:45, September 20, 2014, from
http://en.wikipedia.org/w/index.php?title=Carrie_(novel)&oldid=625555042

Rudyard Kipling. (2014, September 13). In *Wikipedia, The Free Encyclopedia*. Retrieved 20:46, September 20, 2014, from
http://en.wikipedia.org/w/index.php?title=Rudyard_Kipling&oldid=625389442

John Knowles. (2014, September 1). In *Wikipedia, The Free Encyclopedia*. Retrieved 20:48, September 20, 2014, from
http://en.wikipedia.org/w/index.php?title=John_Knowles&oldid=623756669

A Separate Peace. (2014, August 25). In *Wikipedia, The Free Encyclopedia*. Retrieved 20:47, September 20, 2014, from
http://en.wikipedia.org/w/index.php?title=A_Separate_Peace&oldid=622779117

Jerzy Kosiński. (2014, September 19). In *Wikipedia, The Free Encyclopedia*. Retrieved 20:48, September 20, 2014, from
http://en.wikipedia.org/w/index.php?title=Jerzy_Kosi%C5%84ski&oldid=626246610

Steps (novel). (2014, March 25). In *Wikipedia, The Free Encyclopedia*. Retrieved 20:50, September 20, 2014, from
http://en.wikipedia.org/w/index.php?title=Steps_(novel)&oldid=601221008

http://hoaxes.org/archive/permalink/the_steps_experiment
Louis L'Amour. (2014, September 10). In *Wikipedia, The Free Encyclopedia*. Retrieved 21:39, September 20, 2014, from
http://en.wikipedia.org/w/index.php?title=Louis_L%27Amour&oldid=625010828

D. H. Lawrence. (2014, September 14). In *Wikipedia, The Free Encyclopedia*. Retrieved 21:40, September 20, 2014, from
http://en.wikipedia.org/w/index.php?title=D._H._Lawrence&oldid=625486635

http://content.time.com/time/magazine/article/0,9171,738937,00.html

http://www.imdb.com/name/nm0492692/bio

Lady Chatterley's Lover. (2014, June 4). In *Wikipedia, The Free Encyclopedia*. Retrieved 21:42, September 20, 2014, from
http://en.wikipedia.org/w/index.php?title=Lady_Chatterley%27s_Lover&oldid=611514489

http://www.theguardian.com/books/2013/apr/12/john-le-carre-spy-anniversary

John le Carré. (2014, September 17). In *Wikipedia, The Free Encyclopedia*. Retrieved 21:45, September 20, 2014, from
http://en.wikipedia.org/w/index.php?title=John_le_Carr%C3%A9&oldid=625978469

The Spy Who Came in from the Cold. (2014, August 3). In *Wikipedia, The Free Encyclopedia*. Retrieved 21:47, September 20, 2014, from
http://en.wikipedia.org/w/index.php?title=The_Spy_Who_Came_in_from_the_Cold&oldid=619665384

Ursula K. Le Guin. (2014, September 20). In *Wikipedia, The Free Encyclopedia*. Retrieved 21:48, September 20, 2014, from
http://en.wikipedia.org/w/index.php?title=Ursula_K._Le_Guin&oldid=626347254

The Left Hand of Darkness. (2014, September 13). In *Wikipedia, The Free Encyclopedia*. Retrieved 21:58, September 20, 2014, from
http://en.wikipedia.org/w/index.php?title=The_Left_Hand_of_Darkness&oldid=625395227

A Wrinkle in Time. (2014, September 17). In *Wikipedia, The Free Encyclopedia*. Retrieved 22:17, September 20, 2014, from
http://en.wikipedia.org/w/index.php?title=A_Wrinkle_in_Time&oldid=625894011

Jack London. (2014, September 17). In *Wikipedia, The Free Encyclopedia*. Retrieved 22:18, September 20, 2014, from
http://en.wikipedia.org/w/index.php?title=Jack_London&oldid=626003167

http://jacklondonpark.com/jack-london-museum.html

http://books.google.com/books?id=0Sg5AAAAQBAJ&pg=PA81&lpg=PA81&dq=Literally+and+literarily+I+was+saved.%22&source=bl&ots=VhCpsBhQxb&sig=Fh_URRfO6kqUX0Wm63KOJggfauU&hl=en&sa=X&ei=YcT_U7riEsmrigLkzYH4Dg&ved=0CCIQ6AEwAA#v=onepage&q=Literally%20and%20literarily%20I%20was%20saved.%22&f=false

Robert Ludlum. (2014, September 8). In *Wikipedia, The Free Encyclopedia*. Retrieved 22:20, September 20, 2014, from
http://en.wikipedia.org/w/index.php?title=Robert_Ludlum&oldid=624693113

http://www.enotes.com/topics/robert-ludlum

A River Runs Through It (novel). (2014, August 24). In *Wikipedia, The Free Encyclopedia*. Retrieved 22:23, September 20, 2014, from
http://en.wikipedia.org/w/index.php?title=A_River_Runs_Through_It_(novel)&oldid=622632654

http://www.spokesmanreview.com/interactive/bookclub/interviews/interview.asp?IntID=47
http://books.google.com/books?id=dosXQRp7itAC&pg=PA178&lpg=PA178&dq=river+through+it+knopf+rejection&source=bl&ots=NmhESivNNf&sig=8M0tQ5blm1ca04aKpM6RP7JkC08&hl=en&sa=X&ei=7tn_U-m8HYrNiwLL7oFA&ved=0CDkQ6AEwAw#v=onepage&q=river%20through%20it%20knopf%20rejection&f=false

http://www.lettersofnote.com/2012/04/end-of-world-of-books.html

Norman Mailer. (2014, September 18). In *Wikipedia, The Free Encyclopedia*. Retrieved 22:29, September 20, 2014, from
http://en.wikipedia.org/w/index.php?title=Norman_Mailer&oldid=626046446

Life of Pi. (2014, September 10). In *Wikipedia, The Free Encyclopedia*. Retrieved 22:32, September 20, 2014, from
http://en.wikipedia.org/w/index.php?title=Life_of_Pi&oldid=624974609

http://www.theguardian.com/uk/2002/oct/24/bookerprize2002.awardsandprizes

Peter Matthiessen. (2014, September 18). In *Wikipedia, The Free Encyclopedia*. Retrieved 22:33, September 20, 2014, from http://en.wikipedia.org/w/index.php?title=Peter_Matthiessen&oldid=626126097

http://muse.jhu.edu/journals/missouri_review/summary/v023/23.3.article.html

http://norman.hrc.utexas.edu/fasearch/findingaid.cfm?eadid=00301p1

http://flavorwire.com/232203/famous-authors-harshest-rejection-letters#2

W. Somerset Maugham. (2014, August 26). In *Wikipedia, The Free Encyclopedia*. Retrieved 22:38, September 20, 2014, from http://en.wikipedia.org/w/index.php?title=W._Somerset_Maugham&oldid=622896549

Herman Melville. (2014, September 19). In *Wikipedia, The Free Encyclopedia*. Retrieved 22:39, September 20, 2014, from http://en.wikipedia.org/w/index.php?title=Herman_Melville&oldid=626192257

http://www.melville.org/hmmoby.htm#Contemporary

Moby-Dick. (2014, September 19). In *Wikipedia, The Free Encyclopedia*. Retrieved 22:39, September 20, 2014, from http://en.wikipedia.org/w/index.php?title=Moby-Dick&oldid=626164232

Twilight (series). (2014, September 15). In *Wikipedia, The Free Encyclopedia*. Retrieved 22:42, September 20, 2014, from http://en.wikipedia.org/w/index.php?title=Twilight_(series)&oldid=625643719

Stephenie Meyer. (2014, September 15). In *Wikipedia, The Free Encyclopedia*. Retrieved 22:42, September 20, 2014, from http://en.wikipedia.org/w/index.php?title=Stephenie_Meyer&oldid=625658319

http://web.archive.org/web/20091019011138/http://www.publishersweekly.com/article/CA6559505.html

Arthur Miller. (2014, September 20). In *Wikipedia, The Free Encyclopedia*. Retrieved 22:50, September 20, 2014, from http://en.wikipedia.org/w/index.php?title=Arthur_Miller&oldid=626323391

http://www.wga.org/writtenby/writtenbysub.aspx?id=835

Death of a Salesman. (2014, September 10). In *Wikipedia, The Free Encyclopedia*. Retrieved 22:51, September 20, 2014, from http://en.wikipedia.org/w/index.php?title=Death_of_a_Salesman&oldid=624960259

http://books.google.com/books?id=KgIBAwAAQBAJ&pg=PA130&lpg=PA130&dq=%E2%80%9CIf+it%E2%80%99s+going+to+fail,+let+it+fail+the+way+I+wrote+it,+rather+than+the+way+I+rewrote+it.%E2%80%9D&source=bl&ots=7Glqr_zHJ7&sig=MpCZLPAQ8EgrFOhnNfZR6FFbXJQ&hl=en&sa=X&ei=jwYAVO_QFOOHjALmmID4DQ&ved=0CC8Q6AEwAg#v=onepage&q=%E2%80%9CIf%20it%E2%80%99s%20going%20to%20fail%2C%20let%20it%20fail%20the%20way%20I%20wrote%20it%2C%20rather%20than%20the%20way%20I%20rewrote%20it.%E2%80%9D&f=false

Anne of Green Gables. (2014, September 7). In *Wikipedia, The Free Encyclopedia*. Retrieved 22:53, September 20, 2014, from http://en.wikipedia.org/w/index.php?title=Anne_of_Green_Gables&oldid=624487616

Walter Mosley. (2014, June 17). In *Wikipedia, The Free Encyclopedia*. Retrieved 22:56, September 20, 2014, from http://en.wikipedia.org/w/index.php?title=Walter_Mosley&oldid=613285406

Alice Munro. (2014, September 10). In *Wikipedia, The Free Encyclopedia*. Retrieved 22:57, September 20, 2014, from http://en.wikipedia.org/w/index.php?title=Alice_Munro&oldid=624935217

http://www.nytimes.com/2007/09/09/books/review/Oshinsky-t.html?pagewanted=print&_r=1&
Lolita. (2014, September 8). In *Wikipedia, The Free Encyclopedia*. Retrieved 23:07, September 20, 2014, from http://en.wikipedia.org/w/index.php?title=Lolita&oldid=624715110

Vladimir Nabokov. (2014, September 13). In *Wikipedia, The Free Encyclopedia*. Retrieved 23:07, September 20, 2014, from http://en.wikipedia.org/w/index.php?title=Vladimir_Nabokov&oldid=625378713

The Time Traveler's Wife. (2014, September 17). In *Wikipedia, The Free Encyclopedia*. Retrieved 23:12, September 20, 2014, from http://en.wikipedia.org/w/index.php?title=The_Time_Traveler%27s_Wife&oldid=625916263

http://www.nytimes.com/2009/03/11/books/11niff.html?_r=2&ref=arts&

What Was Lost. (2013, August 20). In *Wikipedia, The Free Encyclopedia*. Retrieved 23:14, September 20, 2014, from http://en.wikipedia.org/w/index.php?title=What_Was_Lost&oldid=569329516

George Orwell. (2014, September 19). In *Wikipedia, The Free Encyclopedia*. Retrieved 23:15, September 20, 2014, from http://en.wikipedia.org/w/index.php?title=George_Orwell&oldid=626193739

http://www.wired.com/2014/01/sundance-free-fail-instagram/

http://www.telegraph.co.uk/culture/books/booknews/10877825/The-rejection-letters-how-publishers-snubbed-11-great-authors.html

http://www.openculture.com/2013/11/t-s-eliot-rejects-george-orwells-animal-farm.html

Chuck Palahniuk. (2014, September 15). In *Wikipedia, The Free Encyclopedia*. Retrieved 23:27, September 20, 2014, from
http://en.wikipedia.org/w/index.php?title=Chuck_Palahniuk&oldid=625715790

http://www.salon.com/2003/08/20/palahniuk_3/

http://www.salon.com/2003/08/26/chuck_3/

James Patterson. (2014, September 18). In *Wikipedia, The Free Encyclopedia*. Retrieved 23:30, September 20, 2014, from
http://en.wikipedia.org/w/index.php?title=James_Patterson&oldid=626046279

http://www.today.com/books/fight-what-you-believe-how-best-selling-authors-battled-rejection-6C10971491

Peter Principle. (2014, September 19). In *Wikipedia, The Free Encyclopedia*. Retrieved 23:31, September 20, 2014, from
http://en.wikipedia.org/w/index.php?title=Peter_Principle&oldid=626205319

Harold Pinter. (2014, September 13). In *Wikipedia, The Free Encyclopedia*. Retrieved 23:33, September 20, 2014, from
http://en.wikipedia.org/w/index.php?title=Harold_Pinter&oldid=625416553

http://www.thestage.co.uk/news/2008/04/50th-anniversary-staging-of-the-birthday-party-to-star-hancock/

http://en.wikipedia.org/w/index.php?title=Special:Cite&page=Zen_and_the_Art_of_Motorcycle_Maintenance&id=621911411

http://www.theguardian.com/books/2006/nov/19/fiction

Sylvia Plath. (2014, September 20). In *Wikipedia, The Free Encyclopedia*. Retrieved 23:35, September 20, 2014, from
http://en.wikipedia.org/w/index.php?title=Sylvia_Plath&oldid=626377204

http://flavorwire.com/232203/famous-authors-harshest-rejection-letters

Edgar Allan Poe. (2014, September 10). In *Wikipedia, The Free Encyclopedia*. Retrieved 23:39, September 20, 2014, fromhttp://en.wikipedia.org/w/index.php?title=Edgar_Allan_Poe&oldid=624968322

The Tale of Peter Rabbit. (2014, August 5). In *Wikipedia, The Free Encyclopedia*. Retrieved 23:41, September 20, 2014, from http://en.wikipedia.org/w/index.php?title=The_Tale_of_Peter_Rabbit&oldid=620020816

http://www.poetryfoundation.org/poem/174182

Ezra Pound. (2014, September 18). In *Wikipedia, The Free Encyclopedia*. Retrieved 23:43, September 20, 2014, from http://en.wikipedia.org/w/index.php?title=Ezra_Pound&oldid=626113957

Hugh Prather. (2014, April 29). In *Wikipedia, The Free Encyclopedia*. Retrieved 23:43, September 20, 2014, from http://en.wikipedia.org/w/index.php?title=Hugh_Prather&oldid=606355700

Marcel Proust. (2014, September 16). In *Wikipedia, The Free Encyclopedia*. Retrieved 23:44, September 20, 2014, from http://en.wikipedia.org/w/index.php?title=Marcel_Proust&oldid=625848456

In Search of Lost Time. (2014, September 17). In *Wikipedia, The Free Encyclopedia*. Retrieved 23:46, September 20, 2014, from http://en.wikipedia.org/w/index.php?title=In_Search_of_Lost_Time&oldid=625915089

Ayn Rand. (2014, September 19). In *Wikipedia, The Free Encyclopedia*. Retrieved 23:48, September 20, 2014, from http://en.wikipedia.org/w/index.php?title=Ayn_Rand&oldid=626246043

Call It Sleep. (2014, September 18). In *Wikipedia, The Free Encyclopedia*. Retrieved 23:49, September 20, 2014, from http://en.wikipedia.org/w/index.php?title=Call_It_Sleep&oldid=626061531

http://www.theguardian.com/books/booksblog/2009/sep/07/portnoys-complaint-shocking-49

Portnoy's Complaint. (2014, June 1). In *Wikipedia, The Free Encyclopedia*. Retrieved 23:51, September 20, 2014, from http://en.wikipedia.org/w/index.php?title=Portnoy%27s_Complaint&oldid=611150607

J. K. Rowling. (2014, September 19). In *Wikipedia, The Free Encyclopedia*. Retrieved 23:53, September 20, 2014, from http://en.wikipedia.org/w/index.php?title=J._K._Rowling&oldid=626188771

Harry Potter. (2014, September 12). In *Wikipedia, The Free Encyclopedia*. Retrieved 23:54, September 20, 2014, from
http://en.wikipedia.org/w/index.php?title=Harry_Potter&oldid=625254844

http://www.telegraph.co.uk/culture/books/booknews/9129981/Forbes-list-JK-Rowling-fortune-under-vanishing-spell.html

http://news.harvard.edu/gazette/story/2008/06/text-of-j-k-rowling-speech/

J. D. Salinger. (2014, September 19). In *Wikipedia, The Free Encyclopedia*. Retrieved 23:56, September 20, 2014, from
http://en.wikipedia.org/w/index.php?title=J._D._Salinger&oldid=626161399

http://edition.cnn.com/2008/SHOWBIZ/03/23/rowling.depressed/index.html

The Catcher in the Rye. (2014, September 18). In *Wikipedia, The Free Encyclopedia*. Retrieved 23:57, September 20, 2014, from
http://en.wikipedia.org/w/index.php?title=The_Catcher_in_the_Rye&oldid=626076409

http://www.newyorker.com/magazine/2001/10/01/holden-at-fifty

William Saroyan. (2014, August 29). In *Wikipedia, The Free Encyclopedia*. Retrieved 00:00, September 21, 2014, from
http://en.wikipedia.org/w/index.php?title=William_Saroyan&oldid=623359449

Charles M. Schulz. (2014, September 2). In *Wikipedia, The Free Encyclopedia*. Retrieved 00:01, September 21, 2014, from
http://en.wikipedia.org/w/index.php?title=Charles_M._Schulz&oldid=623818526

http://www.theguardian.com/books/2008/oct/11/peanuts-matt-groening-jonathan-franzen

http://www.turnbacktogod.com/story-of-charles-schulz/

Dr. Seuss. (2014, September 17). In *Wikipedia, The Free Encyclopedia*. Retrieved 00:02, September 21, 2014, from
http://en.wikipedia.org/w/index.php?title=Dr._Seuss&oldid=625943444

And to Think That I Saw It on Mulberry Street. (2014, August 9). In *Wikipedia, The Free Encyclopedia*. Retrieved 00:03, September 21, 2014, from
http://en.wikipedia.org/w/index.php?title=And_to_Think_That_I_Saw_It_on_Mulberry_Street&oldid=620475290

George Bernard Shaw. (2014, September 15). In *Wikipedia, The Free Encyclopedia*. Retrieved 00:04, September 21, 2014, from
http://en.wikipedia.org/w/index.php?title=George_Bernard_Shaw&oldid=625703803

Frankenstein. (2014, September 16). In *Wikipedia, The Free Encyclopedia*. Retrieved 00:04, September 21, 2014, from
http://en.wikipedia.org/w/index.php?title=Frankenstein&oldid=625783490

Mary Shelley. (2014, September 4). In *Wikipedia, The Free Encyclopedia*. Retrieved 00:05, September 21, 2014, from
http://en.wikipedia.org/w/index.php?title=Mary_Shelley&oldid=624133293

http://www.shmoop.com/percy-bysshe-shelley/timeline.html

Shel Silverstein. (2014, September 9). In *Wikipedia, The Free Encyclopedia*. Retrieved 00:06, September 21, 2014, from
http://en.wikipedia.org/w/index.php?title=Shel_Silverstein&oldid=624803103

The Giving Tree. (2014, August 31). In *Wikipedia, The Free Encyclopedia*. Retrieved 00:08, September 21, 2014, from
http://en.wikipedia.org/w/index.php?title=The_Giving_Tree&oldid=623532634

http://www.nytimes.com/books/98/03/22/reviews/980322.22sinklet.html

The Jungle. (2014, September 16). In *Wikipedia, The Free Encyclopedia*. Retrieved 00:11, September 21, 2014, from
http://en.wikipedia.org/w/index.php?title=The_Jungle&oldid=625845435

Upton Sinclair. (2014, September 18). In *Wikipedia, The Free Encyclopedia*. Retrieved 00:11, September 21, 2014, from
http://en.wikipedia.org/w/index.php?title=Upton_Sinclair&oldid=626046582

Satan in Goray. (2014, March 7). In *Wikipedia, The Free Encyclopedia*. Retrieved 00:12, September 21, 2014, from
http://en.wikipedia.org/w/index.php?title=Satan_in_Goray&oldid=598536833

Isaac Bashevis Singer. (2014, September 16). In *Wikipedia, The Free Encyclopedia*. Retrieved 00:13, September 21, 2014, from
http://en.wikipedia.org/w/index.php?title=Isaac_Bashevis_Singer&oldid=625763718

The Notebook (novel). (2014, July 22). In *Wikipedia, The Free Encyclopedia*. Retrieved 00:15, September 21, 2014, from
http://en.wikipedia.org/w/index.php?title=The_Notebook_(novel)&oldid=617958611

The Art of Racing in the Rain. (2014, May 28). In *Wikipedia, The Free Encyclopedia*. Retrieved 00:17, September 21, 2014, from
http://en.wikipedia.org/w/index.php?title=The_Art_of_Racing_in_the_Rain&oldid=610445610

http://www.authormagazine.org/editors_blog/?tag=garth-stein

John Steinbeck. (2014, September 20). In *Wikipedia, The Free Encyclopedia*. Retrieved 00:19, September 21, 2014, from
http://en.wikipedia.org/w/index.php?title=John_Steinbeck&oldid=626379685

http://www.more.com/kathryn-stockett-help-best-seller

The Help. (2014, September 17). In *Wikipedia, The Free Encyclopedia*. Retrieved 00:21, September 21, 2014, from
http://en.wikipedia.org/w/index.php?title=The_Help&oldid=625925147

Lust for Life (novel). (2014, August 26). In *Wikipedia, The Free Encyclopedia*. Retrieved 00:23, September 21, 2014, from
http://en.wikipedia.org/w/index.php?title=Lust_for_Life_(novel)&oldid=622931704

Valley of the Dolls. (2014, September 18). In *Wikipedia, The Free Encyclopedia*. Retrieved 00:26, September 21, 2014, from
http://en.wikipedia.org/w/index.php?title=Valley_of_the_Dolls&oldid=626099314

http://www.onehundredrejections.com/2012/05/rejection-72-jacqueline-susann.html

Henry David Thoreau. (2014, September 18). In *Wikipedia, The Free Encyclopedia*. Retrieved 00:29, September 21, 2014, from
http://en.wikipedia.org/w/index.php?title=Henry_David_Thoreau&oldid=626074086

Walden. (2014, September 20). In *Wikipedia, The Free Encyclopedia*. Retrieved 00:29, September 21, 2014,
from http://en.wikipedia.org/w/index.php?title=Walden&oldid=626327952

John Kennedy Toole. (2014, August 20). In *Wikipedia, The Free Encyclopedia*. Retrieved 00:31, September 21, 2014, from
http://en.wikipedia.org/w/index.php?title=John_Kennedy_Toole&oldid=622041991

http://www.goodreads.com/topic/show/799326-john-kennedy-toole

A Confederacy of Dunces. (2014, September 10). In *Wikipedia, The Free Encyclopedia*. Retrieved 00:31, September 21, 2014, from
http://en.wikipedia.org/w/index.php?title=A_Confederacy_of_Dunces&oldid=624896047

The Color Purple. (2014, September 12). In *Wikipedia, The Free Encyclopedia*. Retrieved 00:32, September 21, 2014, from
http://en.wikipedia.org/w/index.php?title=The_Color_Purple&oldid=625214816

http://aalbc.com/reviews/so_you_wanna_write_a_best_seller.htm

http://www.jason-wallace.com/

H. G. Wells. (2014, September 8). In *Wikipedia, The Free Encyclopedia*. Retrieved 00:35, September 21, 2014, from http://en.wikipedia.org/w/index.php?title=H._G._Wells&oldid=624651245

Leaves of Grass. (2014, September 20). In *Wikipedia, The Free Encyclopedia*. Retrieved 00:36, September 21, 2014, from http://en.wikipedia.org/w/index.php?title=Leaves_of_Grass&oldid=626295962

E. B. White. (2014, July 25). In *Wikipedia, The Free Encyclopedia*. Retrieved 00:37, September 21, 2014, from http://en.wikipedia.org/w/index.php?title=E._B._White&oldid=618356584

Stuart Little. (2014, August 31). In *Wikipedia, The Free Encyclopedia*. Retrieved 00:39, September 21, 2014, from http://en.wikipedia.org/w/index.php?title=Stuart_Little&oldid=623638704

Anne Carroll Moore. (2014, July 17). In *Wikipedia, The Free Encyclopedia*. Retrieved 00:40, September 21, 2014, from http://en.wikipedia.org/w/index.php?title=Anne_Carroll_Moore&oldid=617315681

Charlotte's Web. (2014, September 14). In *Wikipedia, The Free Encyclopedia*. Retrieved 00:41, September 21, 2014, from http://en.wikipedia.org/w/index.php?title=Charlotte%27s_Web&oldid=625473438

Oscar Wilde. (2014, September 18). In *Wikipedia, The Free Encyclopedia*. Retrieved 00:43, September 21, 2014, from http://en.wikipedia.org/w/index.php?title=Oscar_Wilde&oldid=626079503

Look Homeward, Angel. (2014, April 28). In *Wikipedia, The Free Encyclopedia*. Retrieved 00:44, September 21, 2014, from http://en.wikipedia.org/w/index.php?title=Look_Homeward,_Angel&oldid=606218556

The Shack. (2014, September 9). In *Wikipedia, The Free Encyclopedia*. Retrieved 00:45, September 21, 2014, from http://en.wikipedia.org/w/index.php?title=The_Shack&oldid=624837659

General Sources:

http://archive.org/web/

http://www.theatlantic.com/entertainment/archive/2011/11/famous-authors-harshest-rejection-letters/248705/

Bernard, A. (1991). *Rotten rejections: A literary companion*. New York, N.Y., U.S.A.: Penguin Books.

List of best-selling books. (2014, September 18). In *Wikipedia, The Free Encyclopedia*. Retrieved 02:48, September 21, 2014, from http://en.wikipedia.org/w/index.php?title=List_of_best-selling_books&oldid=626074985

http://www.slideshare.net/bright9977/60-famous-failure

http://norman.hrc.utexas.edu/fasearch/findingaid.cfm?eadid=00301p1

http://www.lettersofnote.com/

National Book Award for Fiction. (2014, August 27). In *Wikipedia, The Free Encyclopedia*. Retrieved 02:58, September 21, 2014, from http://en.wikipedia.org/w/index.php?title=National_Book_Award_for_Fiction&oldid=623104253

New York Society for the Suppression of Vice. (2014, May 20). In *Wikipedia, The Free Encyclopedia*. Retrieved 02:51, September 21, 2014, from http://en.wikipedia.org/w/index.php?title=New_York_Society_for_the_Suppression_of_Vice&oldid=609403681

http://www.tyjustwrite.com/blog/famous-authors-harshest-rejection-letters/

http://web.archive.org/web/20060925202706/http://nobelprize.org/contact/faq/index.html#3b

http://www.onehundredrejections.com/

http://www.pulitzer.org/

Made in the USA
Lexington, KY
12 February 2017